# AFRICA
## Around the Edges

Footloose Geezers Vol. III

By Allan D. Brown

ABCOM PUBLISHING

**Africa: Around the Edges**
Footloose Geezers Vol II

Copyright 2020 **Allan Brown**

All rights reserved by the author. No part of this publication may be reproduced, stored in a retrieval system or transmitted in any form or by any means electronic, mechanical, photocopying, recording or otherwise without the prior written permission of the author.

**ISBN: 978-0-578-69752-9**

# ALSO BY ALLAN BROWN

NEWS-DAZE (2006) A novel

BERKELEY-DAZE:
Memoir of a Frat Boy (2007)

SUN-STRUCK:
Growing up in Postwar California (2008)

CALIFORNIA SPLIT:
Racing through the Sixties (2009)

FOOTLOOSE GEEZERS:
Travels through Europe & Down Under
(2013)

AIX—'61: FRAT BOY GOES TO FRANCE:
An Approximate Memoir (2017)

BOSTON BAKED (2018):
Adventures in TV News & Other Exploits


All are available on Lulu.com

**Dedicated to those with wanderlust at any age.**

# PREFACE

**Africa: Around the Edges** describes two tours we took of Africa, one of Southern Africa, the classic safari tour in 2018 and a year later an extensive tour of Egypt in 2019. While admittedly, this covers only a fraction of what Africa had to offer, I felt the two tours did give us an insight into the dramatic contrast between the north and south of the African continent.

As is generally known, Africa is the second-largest continent on the earth after Asia and probably the most diverse in terms of culture and civilizations including the Egyptian civilization which was inextricably linked to the rest of Africa in so many ways including as a source for riches.

So with that happy reading.

# CHAPTERS

## PART ONE: SOUTHERN AFRICA

1. INTRODUCTION ............................................................................ 1

2. TRAVEL AGENT ........................................................................... 8

3. DEPARTURE ................................................................................ 13

4. BOTSWANA ................................................................................. 16

5. ZIMBABWE .................................................................................. 33

6. VICTORIA FALLS ........................................................................ 43

7. NAMIBIA ...................................................................................... 56

8. ETOSHA ....................................................................................... 67

9. SWAKOPMUND ............................................................................ 87

10. SOSSUSVLEI .............................................................................. 95

11. DUNES ...................................................................................... 105

12. WINDHOEK ............................................................................... 114

13. CAPE TOWN ............................................................................. 122

14. ROBBEN ISLAND ..................................................................... 134

15. TABLE MOUNTAIN .................................................................. 144

16. WINE COUNTRY ...................................................................... 154

17. CAPE HOPE .............................................................................. 167

AFTERWORD ................................................................................. 176

# PART TWO: EGYPT

A MOMENT ............................................................. 179

1. FLIGHT ............................................................. 181

2. GIZA ............................................................... 185

3. PHILAE ............................................................. 196

4. KALABSHA .......................................................... 203

5. TEMPLES GALORE .................................................... 208

6. ABU SIMBEL ........................................................ 217

7. ASWAN ............................................................. 224

8. KOM OMBO .......................................................... 233

9. LUXOR ............................................................. 242

10. VALLEY OF THE KINGS .............................................. 248

11. CAIRO ............................................................ 262

12. MEMPHIS/ SAQQARA ................................................. 282

13. ALEXANDRIA ....................................................... 293

14. ADEL TOUR ........................................................ 308

15. EL ALAMEIN ....................................................... 327

16. HOMEWARD ......................................................... 340

APPENDIX .............................................................. 344

Upper Egypt Temples .................................................. 348

# PART ONE

## SOUTHERN AFRICA

# 1. INTRODUCTION

For some reason, a small herd of elephants decided to cross the road about twenty-five yards before us as we rode along on a backroad in the Hwange National Park in Zimbabwe. All of the elephants ignored us as they plodded across until one baby elephant began to cross and got upset seeing us so close by. The baby turned toward us and proceeded to make trumpeting noises, flap his ears and then stomp his feet as if to say bug off.

**Angry Baby Elephant**

At first, we thought this juvenile display of aggression was amusing but then the much larger mom came along and did the same thing. Now it was getting serious. Apparently, she also thought we were in her way too; plus her protective instincts kicked in because junior was upset. She trumpeted, wagged her ears and really stomped. The noise was ear-splitting and she looked like she was on the verge of charging. I urged our driver Dohme to get the fuck out of there. He countered, "You can't just run away. You have to sit still for a few seconds, hold your hand up and stare them down."

We did that for a half-minute but still, mom got more and more riled up and looked like she was indeed ready to charge. Dohme finally decided we had had enough and slowly backed the vehicle down the road in reverse. I tried to capture all of this on video but was so nervous that I missed most of the action.

O.K. so we came out this encounter unscathed but I felt it was a close-run thing. In any case, it was just another day of close calls on safari in the heart of Southern Africa. So what were we doing here anyway? Me, who had always been skeptical of touring Africa.

***

It wasn't always that way. I remember as a young kid looking at a map of Africa in our 1940s edition of a Rand McNally Atlas and wondering what all those blank spaces were about. I saw the names of countries like Nigeria, French West Africa, Belgium Congo, Rhodesia, Union of South Africa and one with a weird name called "Bechuanaland." I also could make out some of the major cities like Cape Town, Lagos, Dakar and even Timbuctoo in the middle of nowhere. In fact, a lot of Africa seemed to be situated in the middle of nowhere. Yes, there were many rivers shown such as the Nile, the Congo, the Zambezi and a big lake called Lake Victoria. But most of the smaller rivers seem to peter out into nowhere.

My Dad told me that even though there were a lot of blank spaces on the African map, most of it had been completely explored. Staring at those blank spaces, I wasn't convinced. The other thing that he told was that Africa was really large, the second largest continent on earth and it had a lot of deserts like the Sahara desert. He explained that you could lump the United States and China into Africa and still have room left over.

Well maybe, but what really fascinated me was the jungle part of Africa, like the Congo. I knew something about that because I had seen a lot of Tarzan movies by that time. You know Johnny Weissmuller movies with titles like *Tarzan and his Mate*, *Tarzan and the Amazons*, *The Lost Tribe*. The best part of those movies was how Tarzan swung from vine to vine through the jungle right along with Cheetah, his pet chimpanzee. That looked exciting and I tried it several times in the trees up on a hill behind our house. Of course, it never occurred to me that those vines had been strategically placed for making the movie. I never found anything like it in my trees on the hill. I had to content myself with swinging on a rope that I had attached to one branch and then another. Anyway, I still wanted to go to Africa and see for myself.

Later in the 1950s, I saw a whole bunch of movies about Africa that were a lot more realistic, like the *African Queen* with Humphrey Bogart towing an old steamboat along a shallow river or *Elephant Walk* where you saw a herd of Elephants walking right through a big mansion that was built on an elephant path and featured a scared shitless Elizabeth Taylor fleeing for her life. At first, I thought it was filmed in Africa but I later learned it was Ceylon. However, it was the same deal in Africa with elephants as we discovered when my wife and I and our daughter went to Africa. Elephants don't like anything blocking their traditional pathways.

Then in the early 1960s, I saw *Hatari* with John Wayne and his crew chasing rhinos across a wide plain in East Africa in a big truck and catching them with a rope loop tied to the end of a long pole, something like catching a wild horse.

At one point, a rhino turns and bashes the truck, flipping it and throwing it occupants out. That was Africa to me, wild and free but I also knew Africa had its darker side.

Maureen, a girl at my high school told me her father was being transferred to South Africa to run a Shell Oil refinery. He had been in management at our local Shell Oil refinery in Martinez, California. Maureen wasn't too happy about that since South Africa had a terrible reputation due to its policy of apartheid.

"All those poor Negroes. I have seen newsreels of them working at the mines and living in such awful slums and protesting in the streets. Worse than what we have here. And they can't go where they want and they have to stay in their townships." (Maureen had lived in the South too.)

But Maureen did tell me that her mother was O.K. with all of that because it meant a big promotion for her father and that she would now have servants and probably a nice house with a pool. In other words, they would be living the life of white privilege.

I filed that away in my mind and essentially forgot about it. I would never be going to South Africa anyway. I wanted the jungle and there were no real jungles in South Africa, just scrubby hills and plains as far as I could tell from old National Geographic magazines.

A few years later, in my freshman year at U.C. Berkeley in 1958, I took a more literary approach to Africa. First, I read *Cry the Beloved Country* by Alan Payton, all about the early years of apartheid and a Zulu priest looking for his fugitive son who was accused of murdering a white man. This was a big bestseller in the 50s.

Then I read Joseph Conrad's *Heart of Darkness*. This was the story of a riverboat captain in the early 20$^{th}$ century going up the Congo River to get ivory from a mysterious white trader upriver called Kurtz. When the captain arrives there, he discovers Kurtz has gone native and become the ruler of a local tribe. Also, Kurtz has a beautiful ebony mistress and scores of skulls posted on pikes. The captain retrieves Kurtz because he is now deathly ill and takes him back down the river. However, Kurtz dies on the way first exclaiming, 'Exterminate all the brutes!'" and then with his last breath, "The horror, the horror." Both books were indeed sobering reads.

At the same time, I was taking a course in British Colonial history and I was thus able to keep up on developments currently underway in British controlled Africa. Several African nations such as Ghana and Nigeria had already become independent from Britain. Others were slated for independence in the near future. Our professor stressed the blessings of British colonial rule in Africa by noting that the Brits had built substantial infrastructure and had set up a British proven legal system to say nothing of the hundreds of British Africans who had been educated in England. The same went for the French with their own African colonies.

***

My next marginal encounter with Africa came a couple of years later in 1961 while I was spending a year in Aix-en-Provence, France. The University of Aix-Marseille had a large contingent of French colonial students from Africa. One of them was Madeline. She was the daughter of a French doctor in Madagascar. She was hang-loose, not uptight like many of the French girls. Tall, buxom, with ravishing red hair, freckles and small dark classes that she wore on the tip of her nose giving her a sassy look. She looked me over and called me "Le Grand American," apparently deciding I was worthy of her time.

We spent hour after hour at the *Deux Garcons Cafe* while she filled me in on the glories of Madagascar, the climate, the tropical breezes, the beaches, the exotic mix of French, African, Arab and Asian cultures, the unique wildlife of lemurs, chameleons and various other lizards. Despite all of that, she lamented that it was boring to live there and how happy she was to escape to Aix-En-Provence.

Although she spoke passable English, the result of frequent visits to Kenya and South Africa as well as British tourists coming to Madagascar, we managed to conduct most routine conversations in elementary French, sometimes in bed. But alas, Madeleine had to return to Madagascar in early January because her mother fell sick and her doctor father needed her to help out for a few months.

My other encounter in Europe with Africans came during a two-week ski vacation in Ehrwald Austria. I stayed in a hostel with a bunch of students from Paris. In that group were six or seven African students from the Ivory Coast, all sons of the elite. Sharp dressers, late risers and always ready for a party, none of them skied. Their idea of a good time was to rise around noon, hang out in the cafes and line up the action for the evening. All were musical, playing a variety of instruments and of course, all could dance. The Austrian blondes loved them and hung on them as if they were royalty.

Following my year in France, I came back to Berkeley all hopped up about joining President Kennedy's spanking new Peace Corps with the aim of possibly going to Africa. Since I now spoke decent French, I figured I could be assigned to a French-speaking country like Senegal and teach English. But when I applied at the end of my senior year in the spring of 1963, the Peace Corps said no. We want you to go to English speaking Nigeria and teach French. Shit! That wasn't part of the program for me. I had no choice. I said O.K. since I had other reasons for joining the Peace Corp. The main one was getting out of the draft. The Peace Corps got you a two-year draft deferment during your service. Plus I figured I could continue in graduate school on the dough I earned in the Peace Corps and maybe escape the draft all together because by then I would be 26, the magical age at which they stopped drafting you.

***

In the summer of 1963, I headed off to Peace Corps training camp which began with three weeks in Puerto Rico doing Tarzan stuff and learning to live off the jungle. Bananas anyone? The next month we underwent intensive training at Columbia University in New York.

Many of my fellow volunteers were from the East Coast, although Alex, a hip English major was from Duke in North Carolina. He liked African literature and writing and was fascinated with Lawrence Durrell and the concept of "negritude."

"Look at the first chapter in *Justine*, in Durrell's *Alexandria Quartet*," said Alex. "Dust tormented streets. Beggars and flies. Five races, five languages, five sexes. Lemon-scented skies. Doesn't that put you right into the place?"

"It sure does," I replied, "but people I know who have been there said Alexandria was a shithole now and probably wasn't much better back in the 1930s when Durrell was there."

"Of course Al, but what a wonderful shithole. Anyway, it doesn't matter what it's really like. It's what's in the writer's imagination."

"I prefer Henry Miller's description of 1930's Paris during his down and out days," I said. "He was a bum and a freeloader but he had the right spirit about the place."

"Yes, but Durrell is much more appropriate to our situation now," countered Alex. "He describes Alexandria as the culmination of Africa—a mélange of all the continent's people including the black races of central Africa. Just think of it, Al, hundreds of miles south, across the wind-swept Sahara lies the groin of the continent. Abidjan, Lagos, Accra--a fecund humidity in which strange growths thrive," said Alex waxing poetic.

"I hope not too strange," I responded. "At least I hope they are curable. All this Peace Corps talk about bilharzia, sleeping sickness, malaria and god knows what else."

"Don't worry about it, man. The important thing is to groove on the blackness of it all. Ever read Aimé Césaire on negritude? Or Sartre's *Black Orpheus*? Or perhaps negritude's more popular expression by James Baldwin?"

"Yeah, I read Baldwin's *The Fire Next Time*. I saw him once at Berkeley. He certainly delves into the black experience but it's focused on America and France."

"Doesn't matter. It's all the same thing. Africa is the starting point," Alex insisted. "That's where it's at."

During this time after classes a few of us began hanging out at a beer joint with a group of African graduate students. They were a lively bunch and threw great parties at their luxurious digs which we gladly attended until all hours of the night, dancing the "high life."

The downside of this was that most of the Africans had studied previously in Moscow and were committed to the Communist cause for Africa. The Peace Corps administration got wind of this and told us to stop hanging out with these would-be Commies. Instead, we should attend their rather dull Peace Corps approved parties with their approved Africans.'

We duly ignored such advice and kept on socializing with the "Commies." In the end, this and other issues came back to haunt me and a few others. We were duly deselected out of the Peace Corps for a variety of reasons. The main one being Nigeria had cut the number of volunteers they needed by 50 percent. So the Peace Corp administrators winnowed the flock. Troublemakers and people who didn't follow orders were shown the door with enough cash in hand to fly back from whence they came. Bummer. Now I had the Army staring me in the face.

I did my duty and joined the Army Reserves, was assigned to a PIO unit at the Presidio in San Francisco where I became involved in television production for the 6th Army headquarters. A year later, I went to San Francisco State in TV, Radio and Film and launched my career in TV news with TV stations in San Francisco, Boston and Chicago. All the while more or less tracking developments in Africa throughout the 70s, 80s and 90s. Much of not good except for the end of apartheid in the early 90s and the release of Nelson Mandela.

However, the majority of stories I dealt with had to do with guerrilla warfare in Africa along with various atrocities, corruption, disease and the decimation of the wildlife. Not a pretty place to be news-wise and why would I want to go there anyway since I felt that the early promises of African independence carried on in the grand western style of democracy had all gone to shit.

Now jump to my retirement years in the 2000s where I had traveled and seen much of the world. Much of the world except sub-Sahara Africa. Do I still have to? Yes, ultimately, I felt I did have to. So here is how it went.

## 2. TRAVEL AGENT

In August of 2017, my wife Yvonne and I were having a now or never moment about Africa. Both in our early 70s but both in good health and reasonably fit but wondering how much longer would that last? We had done Australia, New Zealand, Chile's Patagonia, Tahiti and Easter Island. The only other southern continent country we had not visited was South Africa.

Although my youthful enthusiasm about seeing Africa had waned over the years, I had always been curious about Cape Town, the last city on the landmass of the African continent before you hit the Southern Ocean that extended to the Antarctic. Having already seen the southernmost tips of the landmasses in the Southern Hemisphere, namely New Zealand, Chile, and Australia, Cape Town, South Africa would complete the southern landmass journey.

Then there was the issue of the fast disappearing African wildlife. You know elephants, rhinos, lions and such. Even though for years I was convinced that two days at the San Diego Zoo with its faux game park filled with all these critters would suffice for seeing African wildlife. However, there was still that nagging imperative to go see the real thing in the wild while it still existed.

After some more back and forth and a bit of research, we decided to forge ahead and do the Southern Africa thing for three weeks. There would be three of us. Myself, Allan, my wife Yvonne and my adult daughter Vanessa who would pay her own way.

A rough itinerary that I concocted had us flying into Johannesburg first, then on a short flight to Botswana, next to nearby Victoria Falls in Zimbabwe and finally on to Namibia, all to tour the local wildlife parks.

After that, we would spend six days in Cape Town to check out the scene there.

The question I had to settle in my mind initially was should I set up this entire trip on my own or use a travel agent who specialized in Africa? After a bit of research, I discovered that while I could decide on the big picture, like getting cheap flights to South Africa, the small details of interior flights, local transportation, safari lodging, and other on the ground logistics, etc. were beyond me. After all, it was "Africa." I was also imagining an experience something like Paul Theroux's green hell in his book *Last Train to Zona Verde* where incompetence and corruption reigned. Spare us.

Based on a personal recommendation and some research, we sought out Karen Cockburn of the African Travel Center based in Boulder Colorado. We further checked out her website where she had received rave reviews from former clients. Also, since we lived in Pueblo, in southern Colorado, her Boulder location was relatively convenient should we decide to visit her in person.

When I described what we had in mind over the phone, Karen said such an extensive trip would be a grand experience. Adding that most of those who went on safari went for only a week to ten days. We further indicated that we were thinking about doing this in April. Karen concurred saying it was a great time to go. It would be just at the end of the rainy season and the beginning of fall in Southern Africa. Weather should be great, not too hot or too humid. Also, it was a slow time for the safari camps. The most popular time for game parks was June to October, their winter and spring. In any case, Karen said she would do a preliminary check to see what was available at that time.

A couple of weeks later, Karen got back to us saying that our trip did appear doable but that if we were serious it was time to start making reservations at the various safari camps. To do that Karen wanted to know how much we were willing to spend per day on safari. I told her based on my reading of Fodor's African Safari book, something in the range of four to five hundred a day per person. That would include lodging/meals/and driver/guides throughout the safari parks. She said that was a reasonable amount for the safari camps that she had in mind.

After some more discussion, we definitely settled on two weeks of hardcore safari parks in Botswana, Zimbabwe and Namibia. The Namibia portion would also include the sand dunes located in the Namib-Naukluft

National Park. After that, we wanted to spend six nights in Cape Town which would be relatively cheap for a major city.

Karen said all of that was doable and came up with an estimated land cost of $16,000 for Yvonne and me. And $8,830 for our daughter Vanessa. Vanessa was lucky she didn't have to pay more for a single supplement add-on. Anyway, when you added it all up including the cost of our Delta flights to Johannesburg it was the price of a new mid-size car.

As a capper to this discussion, Karen added that she wanted a 30% down payment for the land and interior flight portion of our trip so she could secure the various reservations for safari lodging, tour guides and drivers and for our stay in Cape Town with a couple of pre-paid tours. Of course, we had to sign a contract with all the fine print assuring that we would go through with this trip.

Over the next few months, Karen kept me updated on what she was able to do reservation wise. By December, everything was locked in as we had envisioned it and final payment was due in January of 2018.

\*\*\*

However, before I coughed up the final payment for this venture I drove up to Boulder from Pueblo, Colorado in late December to pay a visit to Karen Cockburn at her office. Basically, I wanted to see her in person and see her operation. Based on her web page and talking to her on the phone, she certainly sounded legit. Still, who really knew in this scam-laden world? Plus, I wanted to meet her in the flesh. She sounded like an intriguing woman.

It turned out Karen had a modest office on the outskirts of Boulder with one assistant. She greeted me warmly like I was a long-lost friend. She was a woman in her fifties, well-preserved, thin and fit in that Colorado way. During a bit of chit-chat, she explained that she had spent many years in South Africa while married to a South African man involved in the safari business. Thus, she assured me that she had great first-hand knowledge of the safari scene.

Then we got down to business about the final itinerary. Karen had already locked in our reservations at the three major safari camps that we were staying at in Botswana, Zimbabwe and Namibia. Reservations that she said were hard to get even seven or eight months in advance. About Namibia, she encouraged us to reserve a charter flight from the town of

Swakopmund, down the Atlantic coast (Skeleton coast) to the sand dunes area. Only five hundred dollars per person.

"Say what?" I reacted, thinking that we had already spent enough dough on this venture.

"It's a flight over the skeleton coast with that you will never forget," she insisted. "You will fly over old shipwrecks, and abandoned mining camps plus see miles of endless wilderness beaches inaccessible by road."

I yielded. I told her to go ahead since it was now merely a drop in the bucket compared to the total cost.

Finally, Karen handed me a reading list of classic books on the various African countries that we would be visiting. She said it would be our homework for the next few months. I had the feeling that she thought I knew little about Africa. However, I soon abused her of that notion as I ticked off the books I had already read about South Africa over the years such as *The Covenant* by James Michener, *Kaffir Boy*, *Cry the Beloved Country*, *Green Hills of Africa* and more recently *Dark Star Safari* and *Last Train to Zona Verde* by Paul Theroux.

I also mentioned that I had Berkeley friends who had been involved in the ANC during the early 1990s. Of course, I added that I had been dealing with the news from South Africa for years in my former capacity as a newswriter/producer for TV news in Chicago. We had covered first hand and in great detail the end of apartheid and the release and rule of Nelson Mandela for the Chicago market. It seemed as if the visits of Chicago's Jesse Jackson and other black leaders to South Africa were endless during the 80s and 90s. Many of which I had to write about and package video for. So I felt I was well versed on Africa.

*\*\**

In early January, we coughed up the last payment for our African trip. The question was would it be worth it? After all, Africa was recently termed "a shithole" to quote our current president, Donald Trump. Based on current news reports, corruption and crime were still rampant in South Africa and Zimbabwe but Karen assured us that none of that would touch us while we were on safari. Further, if we stuck to the main tourist sights in Cape Town, all would be well.

Then there was the issue of actually spotting the disappearing wildlife of elephants, lions, rhinos, etc. I was afraid that they wouldn't get the memo to show up for their scheduled observation. Also, there was another consideration, namely our fellow safari tourists. Based on our experience in earlier travels to Australia and Chile, I had visions of hordes of Chinese or Japanese tourists hogging all the sights and insanely taking photos. This to say nothing of annoying Americans or Germans we might encounter.

The only saving grace was we would be on our own tour with our own drivers who according to Cockburn were completely reliable. Still, I wondered about the economics of this safari business. How does a travel agent make money on something like this? I would imagine they get at least a ten percent commission. When all is said and done, I hope I don't conclude that a couple of days at the San Diego Safari Zoo would have been much the same thing with a lot less hassle and expense.

So in early April after tying down all the myriad details of getting ready like getting shots and malaria medication and procuring a couple of thousand dollars' worth of South African Rands and US dollars for incidentals including tips, off we went.

So was it worth it? Was it worth the price of a new car for a so-called "trip of a lifetime"? Read on for a day-by-day account.

# 3. DEPARTURE

**Mon. April 23**

The first leg of our trip involved flying from Denver to Atlanta, Georgia. It was at the Atlanta Airport where we met up with Vanessa. She had flown in from Salt Lake City and had arrived at about the same time as us in Atlanta.

The question now was what do we do the kill five hours until our overnight, non-stop Delta flight to Johannesburg, South Africa? Somehow, we managed through it by a combination of reading, wandering around the international terminal and having an early dinner and a beer or two.

Perhaps a word here about why we going by way of Atlanta to Johannesburg in the first place. Most flights to South Africa from the U.S. go by way of Europe. Then there can be a layover of many hours before you can get a connecting flight to Johannesburg. Assuming you can get a quick connecting flight from Europe, the whole operation could take 28 to 30 hours of flight time from Denver to Johannesburg.

By flying from Atlanta directly to Johannesburg in a sixteen-hour flight we saved at least eight-hours without any layovers. Ergo: We definitely did not want to go by way of Europe.

Karen was surprised that we had been able to book this flight direct from Atlanta to Johannesburg. It seems it is usually booked months, even a year ahead in advance. I guess I was lucky but I did book and pay eight months in advance. That was a gamble because at that time we weren't at all sure we would go through with this trip. Of course, I did wonder why Atlanta was a non-stop departure point to South Africa. However, as we discovered part of the answer was that there was a high demand for such flights in the South. Why? Well, possibly one reason was that that's where most of the big game hunters came from, especially Texas. Another possible reason was the constant flow of southern Christian missionaries to and from Southern Africa. Then there was the large middle-class black population in the Atlanta area visiting their "homeland." Also, the South apparently had a lot of business interests in South Africa.

Having been on long-distance night flights before, I paid the upgrade to have extra leg-room for Yvonne and me, namely the exit seats. Vanessa did not upgrade and I think she was sorry as she wound up the back of the plane crunched in a window coach seat. Especially annoying to her was the fact that she was surrounded by a loud group of "born again" missionaries hoping to bring "Christian enlightenment" to the natives.

It turned out that Yvonne and I were sitting next to a white South African woman who had just spent three weeks in Birmingham with a Christian relative and who was also involved in religious doings. It seemed like we were on a "Christian Express." Just to shake things up, when this woman inquired as to our denomination, I told her we were born-again atheists. That shocked her so much that she shut up for the rest of the flight.

In general, though, the flight was a long, boring 16 hours. The food was mediocre. Movies on the so-called entertainment center were hard to see on my screen and hear on my earphones. Plus I had seen most of them already. Thus, I spent my time reading off my electronic reader, the Nook and attempting to sleep. Thank God we could stretch my legs.

**Tue. April 24**

We landed at Johannesburg's Tambo airport at 5:30 pm local time the next day, bummed out and burned out. Coming in, the city reminded me of an L.A. sprawl. It appeared to go on forever with a concentration of skyscrapers in the city center. It was said to have a population of over 4-million. Of course, most of that population was confined to the so-called townships of which the largest was Soweto, a township that we did not plan to see. In fact, we were to spend exactly no time in Jo-Berg by design. Cape Town awaited.

After passport control and customs which went impressively fast, we were met by a Rodney who was our local airport guide. He was among a mob of guides all holding signs for their intended passengers. Our sign read "The 3 Browns." Luckily, there were no other Browns in this mob scene.

Rodney was a cool looking cat dressed in elegant casuals. With a clipped South African accent, he smoothly guided us through this maze-like airport, much larger and more complex than any airport that I had ever been through. It also had a reputation for crime and pilfering of luggage.

Pushing our luggage along in a cart, Rodney led us safely to the City Lodge Hotel located at one end of the airport terminal complex itself. This was the ultimate in convenience. No off-site hotel in Johannesburg proper for us.

After getting settled in our rooms, we decided to have a real meal at the hotel and went down to the restaurant. I ordered a burger with fries and a beer. The fries and beer were good (Castle Beer) but the hamburger was strange. The so-called beef tasted and looked strange. At best it was ground up veal at worst it was ground up monkey meat. (Just kidding.) In any case, I stuck to the fries and beer and stole a little salad from Yvonne and Vanessa who had ordered chicken Caesar salad. After dinner, we all turned in early, relieved that we had finally made it after our marathon flight from the U.S.

# 4. BOTSWANA

**Wed. April 25**

We got up around eight or so, somewhat recovered from jet lag and made ready for an 11:45 a.m. flight to Kasane, Botswana, the first leg of our safari trek. The hotel's breakfast buffet was a lot better than last night's dinner with many goodies from which to choose.

While we were eating, I noticed several mid-forty types sitting alone at various tables. They were all tough-looking, very fit Anglos probably South Africans. They struck me as soldiers of fortune types who knew how to kick ass. They were probably on their way north to Angola or Mozambique where things were still unsettled. Of course, all of this was in my own imagination with no way to check out the reality of the situation.

Later, we headed out into this airport maze for our flight. This time we had no guide or help hauling our luggage. Fortunately, we did have a lot to time to find the South Africa Airway counter. After fifteen minutes or so of wandering around somewhat lost, an airport porter intercepted us and took charge. He rolled our luggage to the South Africa Airway counter. Of course, he wanted a tip. I gave him a couple of bucks worth of Rands. He thanked me and then hustled off.

We finally boarded the S.A. flight around 11 a.m. This was a small cramped plane with tiny seats but we managed and settled in. Two hours later we landed at Kasane Airport. Although small this airport was brand new, very sleek and efficient.

Hey, this must be the "new" Africa, I thought. I had read that Botswana was one of the most advanced and modern countries in sub-

Saharan Africa devoid of corruption where the per capita income was about 8-grand a year, a startling amount for Africa.

We were met by a driver holding a sign that said, "3 Browns—Allan, Yvonne & Vanessa." With a minimum of words, he collected our luggage, loaded it into a van and then drove us for about an hour through scrub and bush country to the Chobe Game Reserve.

A few miles farther on we came upon the Chobe Elephant Camp half-hidden under an arcade of towering trees. Even at first sight, it appeared rather luxurious with structures imitating some African tribal village. It was then that we that it really hit home. We were indeed in Africa going on safari.

As we pulled up, we were greeted by four or five staff members singing a song of welcome in their local dialect. Very charming and then after a cool, non-alcoholic welcome drink, we were shown to our tent cabin about fifty yards from the main lodge.

**Tent Cabin**

Upon entering our cabin, we gazed upon a big king size bed draped with mosquito netting. There was an overhead fan but no air conditioning. We were told that this time of year it was cool at night dipping down to the 50s and even in the daytime, temperatures could barely reach the 70s.

Outside on a deck with a view of a waterhole were a few lounge chairs. The inside and outside walls of the bungalow were made out of canvas giving it that tent feel but with wooden support within the walls. In other words a faux tent.

**King Size Bed**

Checking out the bathroom, I notice that it was open to the bedroom with no door. Also, the bathroom had an outdoor shower.

After settling in, we checked out the main lodge. It was indeed spacious and elegantly designed in the proscribed Safari fashion of vaulted ceilings, overhead fans, thatched roof, wood beams and woodwork all in native woods, mainly African teak. Also, leather couches and easy chairs abounded all scattered about on a wide veranda that overlooked the bush and the waterhole. Nearer to the lodge was a small swimming pool that someone later said the wildlife sometimes drank out of.

**Main Lodge**

At 4 p.m. with three hours of daylight left, we went out on our first safari trek. We rode in a truck that had three rows of elevated seats with a canopy top and a windshield that folded down. All of this provided great unrestricted views of the bush and the wildlife.

**Safari Truck**

Our fellow travelers included an Australian couple from north of Perth and a couple from Hawaii.

The action began right away on the drive led by "Ninja" as he called himself. He was our driver/guide. A cool African with self-proclaimed eyes in the back of his head. As we rolled along, Ninja pointed out some of the flora in the park, including extensive forests of African teak. I always thought teak was a rare wood but here it was most common wood and used extensively for furniture making and general construction as we saw at the lodge.

On this short afternoon drive along the Chobe River, we saw scores of baboons wandering about in troops and sitting under trees acting as if they owned the place. I was struck by how human-like they behaved with their family groupings and relatives, squalling at other troops of baboons for territorial intrusion.

**Baboons**

I kept recalling six-percent, only six percent of DNA separated us humans from most baboons considered the least bright of the primate species. It was actually the chimpanzee that came closest with only a two-percent difference except we hadn't seen any chimpanzees yet.

We also saw several giraffes and zebras, a herd of water buffalo, and a pride of lions resting under a tree near a waterhole about thirty yards from us. Yawning and napping, their bellies apparently so full, the lions paid no attention to us or to the various antelope type critters such as the kudos, impalas and elands that grazed nearby. Everybody was snapping photos of lions like mad during this encounter.

**Lion Pride**

We ended this short drive with a "Sundowner." The guide parked at a scenic spot overlooking the Chobe River and set up a bar with offerings of beer, wine, and gin and tonic. As the sun sank lower in the sky, it was all very mellow and a great introduction to safari life.

**Sundowner**

Back at the lodge, we had another round of gin and tonics on the lodge veranda, watching the last glimmerings of the day. I remarked that gin and tonics seemed to be a popular drink around here. Apparently knowledgeable about such matters, the Aussie told me that the tonic water in Africa had much more quinine in it than in the states. After all, have to ward off malaria, don't you know, but it did give the drink much more kick.

Later, after a quick freshening up, we returned to the main lodge and had dinner around eight. It was chicken and rice affair done up in some African way, quite tasty and all washed down with a bottle of South African Chenin Blanc. We were seated with the Aussie couple and the Hawaiian couple. In all, there were about eight other guests at other tables. I judged that lodge was maybe half full.

Later, we discovered that Aussie couple were interesting in their own way. The mister was in shipping in a port city north of Perth. He said he shipped ore from the nearby mines. His wife was a rough-hewn Aussie from the outback but nice if loud. They were on a grand tour of Africa doing the game parks in Southern Africa. Then they would be off to Rwanda to see the mountain gorillas, and finally to Egypt for a float down the Nile to see the pyramids. These Aussies were getting around.

Regarding the Hawaiian couple, Nick was a *haole* who had moved to Hawaii ten years ago. He said he had once owned a string of beauty shops in Arizona and then retired but sometimes did odd jobs on the big island of Hawaii. A nice middle-aged woman was his girlfriend. Nick was a talkative guy. He went on and on about life in Hawaii. He had some great Maori tattoos on his arms and wore Hawaiian shirts. They were here for ten days doing Chobe and the Victoria Falls area.

After dinner, we went to bed early at 9:30 because we had to be up by six for the early morning safari drive at seven. But returning to our bungalow was a project. Although it was only 50 yards off, the hotel staff insisted that all of us be escorted by a guide with a flashlight to ward off any wild beast lurking about, like a lion. So we waited around for the guide to show up with his flashlight who then led us back to our abode. No lions.

Getting ready for bed was also a hassle because of the mosquito netting that was draped all over the place leading to our entanglement until we straightened it out. This netting was probably unnecessary because we hadn't seen or heard one mosquito the whole time while we were here. Safari day one over and out.

## Thur. April 26

The next morning we were up with the birds around 5:30 a.m. Breakfast was at 6:30. First a word here about the bungalow shower. Since the water was solar heated, it was recommended that you showered in the evening. I ignored that warning. I always want to shower in the morning if I am going somewhere all day. So I stepped into the shower in the early a.m. and turned on the faucet. The water started out cold which was expected and then after a few minutes, it turned lukewarm, piss warm as it were. It never did become hot and even turned cold again after a few minutes. That was a real waker-upper. Nonetheless, I persevered and shaved with cold water.

The other annoying thing about this bungalow was that, as mentioned, the toilet was right out in the open in the bathroom with no enclosure. There was no door to the bathroom so one did his business in full view of the other or others. But wait you say. Aren't you married? Yes for years and years but still one likes some semblance of privacy à la commode. I guess in Africa, no one cared if all bodily functions were on display to whomever.

Following our morning toilet, we met up with Vanessa in the next bungalow and hiked over to the dining area as dawn was breaking. No flashlight guide now. I could foresee this escorting service back and forth to our bungalow would soon be an issue. I had my own flashlight and I felt I could guide ourselves. The standard advice is if one encounters a lion or an elephant in your path is to freeze and let it pass. Make no quick or hysterical moves. However such encounters were extremely remote. Most wildlife tried to avoid human encounter.

Breakfast was the standard buffet with various offerings and custom made eggs if you wished. A lot of sleepy heads were about as well, griping about the early hour. I compared this regimentation to being in the Army or maybe at a Boy Scout camp. We were going to have two weeks of this at various safari camps. In addition, this was to be an all-day safari contrary to the usual pattern of going out early in the morning and returning for lunch and then going out later in the afternoon. We would be on the road with a stop for a picnic lunch somewhere.

We got rolling around 7 a.m. as scheduled. It took only fifteen minutes or so to get into Chobe National Park proper and already there was a line of vehicles at the entrance gate. Each vehicle had to stop and check-in and that took a few minutes each. We finally got checked off and drove on into the park.

**Chobe National Park**

A mile or so in, the wildlife extravaganza started. Here is what we saw that morning in order: First, two giraffes fighting each other by swinging their heads and banging the shit out of one another across their neck and upper body.

**Headbangers**

However, this did not last long and we figured it was a dominance fight with the smaller giraffe backing off. We then saw herds of corkscrew horned creatures known as kudus. These creatures were often hunted for their horns.

**Kudus**

Next, we encountered a herd of water buffalo contentedly grazing in the grass. They too had nasty horns but struck me more like domestic cows than anything else.

**Water Buffalos**

Still, the awesome spectacle of nature's urge to procreate was, at one point, on full display.

**Getting It On**

But wait! We soon ran into a male lion and a female lion stalking this particular herd of water buffalo. The male was off in the distance circling the herd. The female crossed the path of our vehicle a bare twenty feet away, paying absolutely no attention to us, in effect encircling the herd from the opposite direction.

**Stalking Lions**

Since this low key pursuit could take hours before a kill, we watched it roll out for about twenty minutes and then moved on.

Around noon we stopped for a picnic lunch at a so-called rest spot. Also, it served as a much-needed bathroom break. Actually, there were no bathrooms only the bush. The idea was to find a bush behind which to conceal yourself but the guide first had to clear it of snakes and other nasty critters before one could do one's business. The phrase that was used for these bathroom breaks was a spot to "stretch your legs." This was a big deal for the women but for the men, most carelessly pissed a short distance away from the truck.

Lunch was cold cuts, potato salad, fried chicken and beer. Nothing special but adequate.

After lunch, driving along we encountered five or six elephants bashing about in the bush, tearing up vegetation and stripping bark from trees about twenty yards off. One looked up, sort of posing for us then turned back to bush bashing. The others simply ignored us.

**Posing Elephant**

Later we drove over to the Chobe River for a cruise on a flat bottom boat. I took one look at the boat which was now empty but would later be filled with other passengers from other game drives and registered my concern with Yvonne.

**Chobe River Boat**

Essentially, I was not enthusiastic about a two-and-a-half-hour cruise crammed on a boat with other passengers with no toilet facilities. Plus Yvonne, Vanessa and I were tired and still jet-lagged. A nap at this point looked awfully good. Thus, we decided to forego the cruise much to the horror of the other guests now filing onto the boat

"How could you not go on this cruise?" was the question. I didn't bother to answer. It was simple. It was late around 3 p.m. and we were burned out. We needed a respite. Ninja drove us and another couple back to camp saying he understood.

Along the way saw several giraffes eating tree leaves nearby. I realized again what beautiful, graceful animals they were as well as generally being very peaceful.

**Giraffes Dining**

Continuing our journey back to the lodge, we also came upon another small herd of elephants with a couple of babies sloshing about in what appeared to be a small, shallow branch off of the Chobe River. They would root among the river vegetation and then snork up water with their trunks and spray it all over themselves or stick their trunks in their mouths and drink it. All of this was about thirty yards off. Our presence didn't bother them as photographed shot away.

**Water Play**

A word here about the critical role of the driver/guides in ferreting out wildlife in these parks. Without them, most self-drive tourists through these parks wouldn't have a clue where to look. Our guide "Ninja" was an ace at spotting wildlife and pointing it out to us. He seemed to have telescopic eyes as well as eyes in the back of his head. Of course, he also an intimate knowledge of the park and knew where a particular species hung out. Also, he communicated with other fellow guides by radio. In addition, he would stop other sightseeing trucks to confer momentarily with another guide as to what was where and what was going on. That's how we found the pride of lions lounging under a tree yesterday in an out-of-the-way waterhole.

Still, many visitors to the park were coming in either private or rental vehicles. A few of them had personal guides but most of the self-drivers merely wandered around with no clue as to what was where. A few of the clever ones would tail a particular sightseeing vehicle like ours while our driver/guide would do the dirty work of tracking down the wildlife. The self-drives were in effect touring the national park on the cheap but still benefiting from the driver/guide's expertise. I noticed that most of the self-drive cars and vans were filled with either Asians or East Indians. Now and then we would encounter a tour bus filled with tourists hogging the road. Passing by we would see scores of cameras plastering the windows while the interior passengers struggled for a view of the wildlife.

In general, all wildlife viewing had to be done from inside a vehicle whether open or closed. The rule was strict. No wandering around on foot except at designated rest areas. The only tourists who could go on foot were those who were on a designated walking tour. Then you had to be accompanied by a guard who was armed with a rifle that could stop any form of wildlife including lions and elephants. This obviously costs a lot of money. Still, once in a while somebody usually from a self-drive would stop the car and get out, searching for a better spot from which to photograph a particular beast. Ninja mentioned how occasionally a tourist on foot got nailed by a lion or a charging elephant coming from out of nowhere.

We returned to camp around four and took a nap in our bungalow, listening to the birds and other wildlife messing about and drinking at the lodge's waterhole. It was then the full realization hit us that we were indeed in Africa and in a very far away place.

***

That night dinner featured kudu. Not bad. It tasted somewhat similar to beef. Yvonne especially enjoyed it partially fulfilling her vow to sample as much local game meat as possible. Along with it, we downed an excellent bottle of South African red wine as we listened to others recount their boat trip. Some were still shocked that we had blown it off. However, the Aussie couple sitting next to us reported that the cruise while pleasant yielded only one submerged crocodile and several submerged hippos. Also a lot of birds and cranes. In other words, we had not missed much.

Also at our dinner table was a new group of guests. Young Germans. They were a lively bunch chattering on in German but when one young lady sitting next to me and asked me about the game park, she spoke perfect English with a perfect American accent. We chatted a bit and then I remarked how great her English was. She said it was nothing. That in fact, most Germans learned English from an early age. Further, English was not considered a foreign language in Germany; rather it was considered a necessary second language. She admitted that she had never been to the United States. Her accent was the result of watching CNN International.

Safari day two over and out.

# 5. ZIMBABWE

**Fri. April 27**

Early this morning we were driven to the Botswana/Zimbabwe border about an hour away from Chobe. A few miles from the border we encountered long lines of trucks, apparently waiting to cross the border. As we approached the border itself, another long line of private cars and vans waited as well. This did not look promising and I recalled Karen saying that African border crossings could be dicey but that she knew a way to get through this one with a minimum of hassle. The trick was not to take your vehicle across the border. Instead, cross as a pedestrian and you avoid all the vehicle paperwork. Karen said she would have another van on the Zimbabwe side waiting for us with another driver that would take us to Hwang National Park. And that was exactly what happened.

Still, we waited in the pedestrian line for about a half-hour before getting to the window of the border custom agent. He was a fat, bored-looking official in a border guard uniform who spent a long time giving us a visa and stamping our passports. Then wanting to chat, he took one look at Vanessa and her single status in her passport and he asked me how many head of cattle would it take for me to offer her up as his wife. I jokingly said, "Two hundred head of cattle or four elephants." He laughed and motioned us to go on.

Outside the border control station, Vanessa burst forth with "How could you, Dad. That was so humiliating."

I apologized but she was still pissed. Luckily, our van and a new guide from the Wild Horizon Tourist Agency was right there on the Zimbabwe side and we piled in. Our bags had already been loaded. So much for an African border crossing by road.

As we rolled along I was beginning to realize that Zimbabwe was not as advanced as Botswana. It didn't look as prosperous. We saw an endless stream of natives walking along the road. Where were they going, I wondered? Our driver said he had no idea. These people were always on the go, he said, possibly on their way to the nearby town of Victoria Falls or to visit relatives. Most were shabbily dressed in cast-off western clothes, T-shirts, flip-flops, dungarees, etc. Some wore Chicago Bulls T-shirts, others had on Obama for President T-shirts. Others had on jogging garb as they jogged along.

**Morning Outing**

A few miles farther down the road, we stopped to refuel at a gas station shaded by giant acacia trees. This was the only gas station for kilometers around according to our guide. The stop in itself was interesting. There were a lot of vehicles scattered about waiting their turn to gas up. Also, a few semi-trucks parked to the side, the drivers in no apparent hurry to move on, many eating their lunch.

There was a snack shop and a mini-grocery store. We went inside the grocery store and purchased several ice cream bars. I was worried about how to pay for it since I had no Zimbabwe money. The guide then told me that Zimbabwe money was no good here anyway. You paid in either South African Rands or US dollars. US money was now the official currency of Zimbabwe.

The other sight of interest to us was a troop of baboons sitting nonchalantly under the shade one of those giant acacia trees with the mothers placidly nursing their offspring. A very peaceful setting. Now and then the dominant males would stroll off looking around the service station grounds for garbage or anything to eat. Nobody seemed to care about feeding wildlife here and in fact, I saw truck drivers throwing the remnants of their sandwiches at them along with some fruit and banana skins which the baboons immediately scooped up. Once again the baboons acted like they were members of a very privileged primate group which of course included we humans.

Moving on after gassing up, it took us about two hours of riding through the Zimbabwe countryside before we came to the Hwange Game Reserve.

**Zimbabwe Countryside**

Most of the countryside was low bush punctuated by various trees, acacia and baobab. Not very jungle-like but rather an open sub-tropical forest.

Our camp, the Hwange Elephant's Eye Camp was right outside the reserve. It too was a luxury camp with all the trappings—cute, tent-like thatched-roof bungalows on stilts with a view of the main waterhole.

**Our Bungalow**

The camp also featured a woodsy main lodge more elaborate than the lodge in Chobe. It also had an elevated viewing deck with a telescope and binoculars for game viewing.

**Hwange Camp**

The food turned out to be rather gourmet and the drinks were endless. Right then we didn't have time for all of that. We had to get out on a late afternoon drive. We were with one other couple. Our driver/guide was named Dohme, a personable fellow, older than Ninja and much more relaxed. Of course, he the prerequisite eyes in the back of his head.

**Vanessa & Dohme**

Our afternoon drive was well-timed because we saw a variety of wildlife all hanging out at a major waterhole—scores of zebras, giraffes and elephants all peacefully drinking or nibbling on vegetation. No sign of lions or baboons. We noticed that the park seemed deserted except for us. No other vehicles were about.

**Hwange Zebras**

*Africa: Around the Edges*

According to Karen Cockburn, this park was much less visited than Chobe or Etosha in Namibia. Part of the reason was it was quite distant from the Victoria Falls area. Also until recently, it was off-limits due to the uncertain political situation in Zimbabwe. Namely the corrupt, terrorist rule of President Mugabe. However, Mugabe was no longer in power in Zimbabwe and we were in only a tiny, far eastern corner of the country.

In addition, Zimbabwe desperately needed tourist dollars. Indeed, their national currency was now the U.S. dollar as mentioned earlier. Their own currency had died in a fit of inflation. Later in Cape Town, I bought a 30-billion dollar bill in Zimbabwe currency which until a few months ago was worth a few bucks U.S. but now was worth nothing. Indeed I paid most of our tips in Zimbabwe in U.S. dollars, some in South African Rands.

That evening we enjoyed another game meal, oryx this time, even more beef-like than kudu. An oryx was another antelope type creature sometimes referred to as a gemsbok.

**Oryx**

We shared a bottle of wine with the only other couple at the camp, a middle-aged British couple from London, David Bachelor and his wife. They had recently married and this was their honeymoon. Bachelor was a roving banker of sorts. He said he traveled the world setting up branch banks for his main bank in London. He had a few stories to tell about what was involved in dealing with third world countries and the crazy world of international banking. The wife was a former co-worker. Both were on their second marriage with grown kids from the first.

Back at our bungalow, we noted that the temperature was dropping fast. No such thing as a heater in this joint. Luckily we had down comforter on the big double bed.

Oh, I almost forgot. Today April 27th was my birthday and still hanging tough. What better place to celebrate it than in the heart of Africa. The big celebration would come in a couple of days later during our stay at Victoria Falls.

**Sat. April 28**

When we woke up the next morning it felt freezing, somewhere around 45 degrees. "What the hell! This is Africa!" That's not supposed to happen! But alas, it does. Maybe it was an elevation problem (2500 feet); also it was fall here.

We got up, showered, (thank god, the water was warm), dressed, and wore our heaviest jackets at the breakfast table because it was still cold. Sharing our table with the British couple, we compared notes on some mysterious nighttime visitors. Vanessa described something brushing by the walls of her tent cabin. We heard that too, a brushing by our tent cabin. Woosh, woosh and, heavy breath. Waking up to this, I didn't know if a lion was on the prowl or what. Even the thought of an elephant passing by was scary. I could easily imagine one puncturing our tent wall with its tusks. In any case, I was too scared to get up and check it out.

After sunrise, we did look around and saw that all the vegetation around our cabin had been crunched down. When we mentioned this to Dohme, he laughed and said it was probably elephants and that they were harmless, just curious and anyway they loved to eat the vegetation around our cabins.

Eventually, we got off in good style for another run through Hwang Park. Even though this was an all-day excursion, Dohme told us we would only be covering a small portion of the park. After all, Hwang encompassed over five thousand square miles, much bigger than Chobe National Park.

Once again we encountered giraffes, zebras, gemsbok and elands along with a jackal or two.

*Africa: Around the Edges*

**Jackal**

Actually, it was a ho-hum outing for most of the day with no sign of lions, cheetahs or leopards. We had a picnic lunch at a rest spot that featured a viewing platform. But there was not much to view other than the antelope type critters like elands and kudus.

Then late afternoon, the real action began. We ran into a large herd of elephants. First up was a lonely bull elephant rooting around in a small waterhole. Dohme said he appeared to be in musth, i.e. looking to get laid. The bull elephant gave us the bad eye as we passed and twitched his ears like we were annoying him.

**Bull Elephant in Musth**

We quickly drove on down the road and eventually came to an even larger herd of elephants with babies in tow.

**Baby Elephant in Front**

They were splashing and sloshing around having a good old time in a large waterhole. Then for some reason, several elephants decided to cross the road about twenty yards before us. As described earlier, all of them ignored us until one baby elephant tried to cross and got very upset seeing us. He or she turned toward us and proceeded to make trumpet noises, flap his ears and then stomp his feet.

**Pissed-off Junior**

We thought this was amusing but then mom came along and did the same thing. Now it was getting serious. She apparently thought we were in her way, plus her protective instincts kicked in because junior was upset. She trumpeted through her trunk, wagged her ears and stomped her feet. The noise was ear-splitting and she looked as if she was on the verge of charging.

I urged Dohme to get the hell out of here. But he countered, "You can't just run away. You have to sit still for a few seconds, hold your hand up and stare them down."

We did that for a minute but still, mom got more and more riled up. Dohme finally decided we had enough and slowly backed the vehicle down the road. I tried to video all of this but was so nervous that I missed most of the action.

O.K. so we came out this encounter unscathed but I felt it was a close-run thing. All of a sudden we and the Brits got tired of wildlife viewing and urged Dohme to return to the lodge early which he did. We then retired to the lounge and had a round of gin and tonics while we discussed our harrowing encounter with pissed-off elephants.

This little encounter made me realize that Hwang Park and its wild critters were much less used to safari vehicles and camera-toting tourists than in Chobe. After dinner, we turned in early wondering if we would once again have some midnight visitors.

# 6. VICTORIA FALLS

**Sun. April 29**

The next morning, it wasn't quite as cold as the night before. Nevertheless, there was a nip in the air as we sipped our morning coffee and devoured our breakfast. The British couple was quite unhappy that they had not seen a lion, a cheetah or a leopard on their prior outings. They had only a week for their safari outing and this was day three. The Brits wanted to know about Chobe implying that they should have chosen that park instead. Dohme told them that all of these critters were about in Hwange but that seeing them was a hit or miss proposition.

In any case, the Brits were hopeful they would encounter the big cats at their next stay in the park which was a real camp with real tents in a more remote location. Also, they would be scouting the wildlife out on foot, i.e. taking a walking safari with an armed escort. I tried to reassure them that they would most likely run into at least a lion or two and maybe get real close, closer than they probably wanted to. We wished them good luck and said goodbye as they were driven off. Now we had to kill time waiting for our early afternoon ride to our next attraction, namely Victoria Falls.

For some reason our ride to Victoria Falls was delayed so we ate lunch at the lodge and then around two, the Wild Horizon ride finally showed up. This irritated me because I had wanted to get to Victoria Falls early and maybe take a short look around at the falls. Anyway, off we went for the two-hour ride to the town of Victoria Falls.

On the way, we came across a dead giraffe in the brush at the side of the road. Our driver stopped and checked it out. It was also being examined by a couple of park rangers. It didn't appear to have been killed by a car or by a lion or leopard. It was quite intact and relatively young. It was a mystery that even the park rangers could not figure out. After a few minutes, we moved on and out onto the major highway to Victoria Falls. Once again we saw endless lines of pedestrians strolling along the highway on their mysterious journeys.

Finally, we arrived around four at the Victoria Falls Safari Hotel which was a huge wood/thatch structure vaguely designed in the longhouse tribal style of Africa with trees growing right through it. Maybe something like a chief of old would live in with his extended family.

**Victoria Falls Safari Hotel**

This was supposed to be the most elegant hotel in the area but it looked dated and slightly tattered around the edges. I suppose all that wood was hard to keep up. Our room was off on a wing from the main building and had a nice view of the woodland around and a local waterhole. But as far as I could see, no view of the falls at least from our side of the hotel.

We chilled for an hour until it was five and then our Wild Horizon guide showed up to take us for a sunset cruise on the Zambezi River. This was something that all of us had been looking forward to. How cool we thought, cruising the famous Zambezi at sunset. Shades of David Livingston! Maybe this would make up for the cruise that we had missed in Chobe. I am glad to report that the cruise did not disappoint.

First, we were greeted by an entourage of tribal dancers doing their African thing.

**African Dancers**

Then we were hustled onto a flat bottom cruise boat that was already set up with a bar and tables and chairs set for dining. Compared to other nearby cruise boats crammed with tourists, we could immediately see that we were on a less crowded boat with a more upscale the clientele. Best of all, drinks were included. Both Vanessa and I started with a gantic gin and tonic. Yvonne had a light beer.

**Zambezi River**

As we settled in, the boat shoved off and into the wide and placid Zambezi. It should be noted that a mile downriver, this placid river would become a raging torrent as it plunged over the falls but we had yet to check that out. Instead, we cruised upriver skirting the banks. At one point we spotted a large crocodile resting its weary bones onshore. Despite a lot of hooting and shouting for an action photo, the croc did not stir. He was like a piece of wood. One well-dressed lady remarked that the croc would make a splendid piece of luggage.

**Zambezi Croc**

The other major sight on the river was a herd of hippos mostly submerged. All you could see were the snouts and sometimes their full heads. Basically, they live mostly semi-submerged.

**Zambezi Hippos**

While all of this was going on, we were drinking and talking to Margo, an Australian lady traveling alone. She had invited herself to our table. Actually, she was a welcome addition to our party and over a dinner of crocodile kabob, we had a lively discussion comparing Australia and Africa. She was smart, worldly, independent and well put together. Her sad story was that her husband of many years had just died six months ago and rather than mope around and mourn, she decided to go off alone on their previously planned trip to Africa. She had guts.

**Allan & Margo**

During our time in Victoria Falls, we were to run into Margo again and again as he hooked up with various other parties. Now back to that crocodile kabob. It did indeed taste like chicken, a rather hardy chicken but seasoned and barbequed as it was, it was delicious.

Soon the sun was setting over the Zambezi, casting an ethereal glow over the waters, making us realize that this was indeed Africa at its finest.

**Sunset on the Zambezi**

After the sun had set, the boat turned up its colored lights and struck up the music in a kind of an African rock. After another round of drinks, we docked, half bombed and were driven back to our hotel where we immediately crashed, realizing that we hadn't missed much by not going on Chobe cruise. Tomorrow, a look at Victoria Falls to see what we can see.

## Mon. April 30

After a fulsome breakfast at the hotel the next morning, we were up and out for a private tour of Victoria Falls by Wild Horizon. We drove over to the main gate to the falls but could see nothing. Yes, we could certainly hear the crashing water but that was it.

In order to see something, we had to hike out onto a jungle trail that followed a ridge overlooking the gorge into which the falls plummeted. Even then there was no full cinemascope view of the falls as there is when viewing Niagara Falls from many different viewpoints.

The problem was the falls were at their peak for the season and the mist from the spray obscured all the views. Only occasionally, could we make out the falls through the mist. Also, we got soaked just standing there trying to take a look. Luckily, we had rented raincoats to keep somewhat dry.

**Victoria Falls**

About two-thirds of the way along this mist soaked trail, Yvonne and I gave up. It was pointless because you saw next to nothing. So we hiked back to a shortcut to the main entrance. Vanessa stuck with the guide and made her way out to that famous bridge over the Zambezi Gorge (Victoria Falls Bridge and Steam Railway.) She deemed it impressive and shot many photos.

**Victoria Falls Bridge**

Meanwhile, Yvonne and I lounged in a café in the sunshine and had a coke while waiting for the guide and Vanessa.

After we regrouped, we decided on the spur of the moment to take a helicopter ride for an aerial view of the falls. This was not too expensive, about $450 for the three of us. It turned out to be a smart move. The chopper was very comfortable, and we three were the only passengers. The pilot, Mike, was a South African in whom we immediately had great confidence. Off we went and soon we were hovering over the falls at about four hundred feet of altitude.

Finally, we had a great view of the falls with the water plunging over the cliffs and into the gorge. The falls now made sense to me from a topographical point of view.

**Victoria Falls Aerial**

There was the wide Zambezi River flowing majestically and peacefully along until it came to the edge of the cliffs, actually, a series of cliffs and then all the water plunged into a narrow gorge with spray flying everywhere. Next, the Zambezi River re-assembled itself into a narrow white water chute for a stretch but eventually flattened out into a peaceful waterway. Mike circled the falls several times during our 20-minute flight and we took all the photos and video we wanted.

I also concluded that while spectacular, Victoria Falls didn't measure up visually in my mind to Niagara Falls. Even though Victoria Falls as more vertical and width than Niagara and has a higher flow rate of water, I felt Niagara was infinitely more scenic and certainly more accessible to the average tourist.

**Niagara Falls**

In addition, nothing beat a ride on the Maiden of the Mist tour boat which skirts the Niagara Falls only a few feet away in all their thundering fury. Needless to say, you get drenched and impressed.

Of course, Victoria Falls has a more glamorous history than Niagara Falls. The locals called it *Mosi-oa-Tunya* which means "smoke that thunders." Dr. David Livingston is believed to be the first European to set eyes on the falls in 1855. He was in a native dugout when he came up to the edge of the falls. As he recorded in his diary "It has never been seen before by European eyes, but scenes so wonderful must have been gazed upon by angels in their flight".

Today Victoria Falls is a world heritage site and noted for having the largest flow of water of any waterfall in the world. It is also listed as one of the Seven Natural Wonders of the World. All right, all very inspiring. I am still with Niagara.

***

Later that afternoon, we went out to a small private game park near the falls (Victoria Falls Private Game Reserve) that specialized in harboring rhinos. With the driver/guide, we spent two hours looking for the rhinos but they were nowhere to be seen. Hiding in the bush somewhere the guide said. At one point he got out of the truck and took off through the bush trying to ferret out a rhino that he claimed he had had a glimpse of. Vanessa and Yvonne followed him for a while despite my warnings to get back in the truck. I stood by the truck, remembering that rhinos are easily pissed off and can attack humans, moving much faster than anyone can run.

Obviously, these rhinos did not want to be seen. The foot trek a bust, all returned to the truck. The guide explained that these rhinos were human shy because many had been harassed by would-be poachers, escaping only because an anti-poacher patrol had scared them off. These anti-poacher patrols were armed with high powered rifles and were authorized to shoot to kill should they encounter a poacher.

Of course, the goal of the poacher was to kill the rhino, cut off the horns and have it shipped it to Asia where it was worth thousands of dollars supposedly to act as a stimulate to limp dicks. I guess the Asians (mainly Chinese and Vietnamese,) haven't heard of Viagra. As a result, black rhinos are on the endangered list.

Finally, ready to give up spotting a rhino, we drove by a ranger station that housed a squad of anti-poachers and there in the parking lot behind a row of parked cars were two rhinos grazing peacefully on the nearby foliage. No fools these rhinos. They had picked the safest spot on the park to hang out, out of danger. We watched for a while from the truck just thirty feet away from the rhinos, snapping photos. The rhinos ignored us, knowing they were safe.

**Protected Rhinos**

We were back at the hotel by six where we chilled and got ready to go out to dine at the nearby Boma Restaurant. This was a restaurant that specialized in African cuisine with a lot of game meat. This was supposed to be my big birthday meal and I dressed up for the occasion with a Hawaiian shirt and light tan chinos.

As we approached the Boma Restaurant which was on the grounds of our hotel, I joked that all they needed was a big "O" in front their name, i.e. OBAMA instead of BOMA to remind us our former president, Obama.

The place resembled a huge African hut with all its thatch and beams overhead and adobe walls. When we entered around seven, everything was already in full swing with ear-splitting African drums and wild dancing with winsome African women in full tribal costume.

**Boma Nightclub**

We were seated in the midst of this chaos by a tall and imposing African server in a Masai warrior costume. We ordered a round of beers and then made our way over to a buffet spread. And what a spread! This was the most wild-ass serve yourself buffet that I had ever seen with dish after meat dish of various game—Ostrich, Kudu, Wildebeest, Hedgehog, Eland, Oryx, etc. This along with other weird vegetables and grains, potatoes and oh yes, if you wanted, a slab of tri-tip beef. Needless to say,

Yvonne filled her plate with the exotic while Vanessa and I kept to our already sampled African game meats with a slice of tri-tip.

After stuffing ourselves, we hung around for the on-going floor show. At one point everyone was invited to get up and dance. So Yvonne got up and danced imitating the tribal steps very well. With her Surinamese background, she always said she was half native. Meanwhile, Vanessa grew tired of the whole scene and her embarrassing mother and excused herself. I accompanied her to the hotel van that was standing by to transport half-bombed guests back to their quarters. I then returned and fetched Yvonne from the proceedings. We strolled back to the hotel clearing our heads in the fresh, cool breeze.

Over and out for Victoria Falls. Tomorrow a flight to Johannesburg and then to Windhoek in Namibia for the third phase of our safari outing.

# 7. NAMIBIA

**Tue. May 1**

After a morning of chilling in the hotel, we vanned it over to the Victoria Falls Airport for our 1:30 p.m. flight back to Jo-Berg. Our ultimate destination was Windhoek, Namibia which was only an hour away by air if you flew directly from Victoria Falls. So why were we flying back to Jo-berg and then changing planes for a flight to Windhoek, thus tripling our air miles? This would an all-day flight ordeal we had to endure.

The kicker was that while there was a direct flight from Vic Falls to Windhoek, it was only four days a week and even then it was constantly being canceled. Karen thought it was better to play it safe and take the indirect route which was a sure thing even if it took all day to get to our destination. She was probably right.

As it turned all the flights went off on schedule and it turned out that Air Namibia was a classy airline with attractive flight attendants and good food. Just like the old days of flying in the 1960s. Anyway, we landed at the Windhoek Airport at around 8 p.m. and there Johnny-on-the-spot was a representative from Ultimate Safaris to ferry us to the Galton Guest Lodge where we were to spend the night.

The first thing the rep. did was to give us a beautiful leather and canvas "man purse" that housed all the documents for the Namibia portion of our trip. This was a total surprise to me because, prior to our arrival, I had no clue as to who or what our week in Namibia was to involve other than sightseeing in the main game park, Etosha and spending a couple of days down in the desert dune area called Sossusvlei.

In fact, I had bugged Karen about this portion of our trip. All the other portions of the trip were fully documented as to hotels, pick up times, tours, etc. and in my hands before we had left Colorado except our stay in Namibia. The particulars of Namibia were a black hole to me other than a cryptic note in one of my original itineraries that an outfit called Ultimate Safaris would be in charge of this portion of our trip. Karen told me not to worry and that we would be in good hands in Namibia. It turned out she was right.

This side note, while waiting for our flight to Namibia in Jo-berg, I had chatted with a fellow passenger who told me he was a guide for some safari outfit in Windhoek and was returning home after driving a few passengers around to all the game parks in South Africa. He was in effect a personal driver/guide for over a week for these folks. I thought that interesting but when we saw him upon landing at the Windhoek airport, he greeted our greeter like an old friend. It turned out that both worked for the same company, Ultimate Safaris. Coincidence? He did tell us that we would be in good hands with this company for our time in Namibia and moved on.

O.K. duly informed, we climbed into the van with our already loaded luggage and were driven into Windhoek about 40 kilometers away. We didn't see much of the town since it was now dark. Judging by the lights, it struck me as a good size city. We finally arrived at the Galton Lodge, a cozy little place on the edge of town that catered to the in-transit guests of Ultimate Safaris. Having eaten well on the plane we immediately went to bed and soon were sound asleep, still wondering what was in store for us on this portion of the trip.

**Wed. May 2**

The next morning we had a pleasant breakfast at the Guest House with the cook whipping of a great omelet. Around nine, a young white guy with a fashionable bush beard showed up and introduced himself as Tarry, (Not Terry) saying he was from Ultimate Safaris that he would be our guide for the entire week that we were there.

"Say what! The entire week! What if we don't get along?" I thought.

I wasn't too sure about this. I had initially thought that this Tarry would simply take us to Etosha, the major game reserve in northern Namibia and dump us there and that we would go out with the local safari guides as we did in Botswana and Zimbabwe.

But no, Tarry, explained that this would be a private, customized tour throughout Namibia of which he proudly proclaimed to be a citizen. He reassured us that he was an expert in the country and that he had been doing this for ten years off and on. Further, he added that he had been promoted to supervisor of all the safari guides in his company and now spent most of his time in the office arranging things. So I wondered aloud how come he was going to spend a week with us if was an administrator.

"It gets boring in the office," he explained. "I had a light workload these next few days so I was itching to get out into the bush. Your family filled the bill for me. Only a party of three. We can do and see a lot."

"Well, O.K.," I said.

Sensing I still had doubts about his escort service, Tarry took me out to check out his company's customized safari vehicle. It was basically a re-configured four-wheel-drive Toyota Land Cruiser with three tiers of seats and large viewing windows. Most of the time this custom made land cruiser was entirely closed in for regular highway travel but in the game parks the roof popped up allowing passengers and the driver to stand up and get a good view of animals, scenery whatever.

As we loaded up and got underway, the van proved to be quite comfortable with leather adjustable seats and plenty of legroom and of course air-conditioning.

**Custom Safari Van**

Since she often got car sick I urged Vanessa to sit up front with Tarry and Yvonne and I sat in the second row. We stowed our backpacks and other luggage in the third row and also in the cargo rear. Also, as Tarry pointed out, the van had radio communication with other safari vehicles and a so-called "Magic Box" which was chock full of food, booze and other goodies to accommodate all needs from a bush breakfast to coffee and tea snacks to majestic gin-soaked sundowners. There was even a side pocket stuffed with a roll of toilet paper in case someone had to take an urgent "bush" number two.

So slowly I was sold on having Tarry as our seven-day guide. But I did warn him that the Brown family was prone to squabbles with everyone wanting to be the boss and dealing with us would be like herding cats. He seemed nonplussed about that saying, "Don't worry I have seen it all and you know my family is something like that. All chiefs and no Indians".

Later he described some of his more bizarre clients like a bunch of crazy Russians, uptight bird spotters and even one cranky old lady that he escorted around Namibia solo. At that point I sensed that he felt comfortable with us, telling us stories out of school about his clients.

As we drove along heading to Etosha about fours off, Tarry filled us in further on his background. He was born and raised in Namibia. He was now twenty-nine, soon to be thirty and had a fiancée, a young lady in medical residency in Pretoria. His parents came from South Africa and Rhodesia (Zimbabwe.) His mother was a geologist who had been working for a mining company in Namibia; his father was in construction and specialized in building resort hotels.

Tarry had gone to a private school in Windhoek where his mother was now a teacher and then went on to the University of Port Elizabeth where he was the only student from Namibia and somewhat of a celebrity. He had majored in Parks and Wildlife management. He spent four years there and returned to Namibia and went into the safari business full time, something he had been doing on and off before.

Tarry struck us as a normal Anglo type raised in exotic circumstances. As we were to find out, he had expert knowledge in the areas of wildlife, birdlife, native life, plants, geology and astronomy. Tarry also spoke four languages: English, Afrikaans, German and the local tribal language. We heard him speak in all these languages and he spoke them fluently.

Then there was the sensitive issue of race relations in Namibia. I bluntly asked Tarry what percentage of Namibia was white. He said about 5 percent out of a population of two-and-a-half million. Windhoek alone had about 326-thousand residents and was growing all the time. He said, of course, the black Africans ran the country but that it was well run, somewhat similar to neighboring Botswana. Tarry claimed corruption was minimal and that Namibia was currently enjoying a boom. Investments were pouring in from overseas and from South Africa and tourism was way up. That in fact, Namibia was one of the wealthiest countries in Africa even though half the population lived below the poverty line. Tarry went on to say he had many African friends and that his company employed quite a few. "Everybody gets along and appreciates the other as far as I can tell. "

Overall, it sounded good, I thought. Maybe too good. I wondered what with all the racial turmoil and tension in South Africa, couldn't that spill over the border into Namibia? But that's another subject that will be explored later on in this account of our trip.

***

We headed north through low scrub and grassland country for mile after mile. Tarry kept exclaiming that the landscape was greener than usual due to a heavy rainy season and was now at its most beautiful. Still, it all looked dry to me. I guess it's what you are used to.

**Namibia Countryside**

After four hours of travel on mostly gravel and dirt roads, we arrived at our destination, the Onguma Tented Camp Lodge. The camp was only a few kilometers from the Etosha National Park entrance. And what a stunning camp it was. At first appearance, far more luxurious than our prior camps.

**Onguma Tented Camp**

After the traditional greeting by the local staff with song and dance, we settled into our tent cabin more upscale than those at Chobe and Hwange except there was no lock on the entrance door, unlike our prior cabins.

**Onguma Tent Cabin**

When I brought this to the attention of Tarry, he said not to worry. This was a very safe and proper camp. There was no theft here. O.K. if you say so but I was still worried about outsiders coming in. I had heard about other camps where tourists had been ripped off. In one case a couple was murdered, something that happened a few years ago in South Africa.

Around four, we were hustled out by Tarry to join a sundowner drive through a private preserve adjacent to the Onguma Lodge. This was put on by the camp itself and wasn't part of the Ultimate Safaris program. On this late afternoon drive, we saw many zebras, giraffes and a few elephants but most interesting to me were the scores of jackals we saw running and rooting around.

These were hearty little, fox-like creatures that could survive anywhere. Because they were scavengers, they could eat anything while other animals starved. They were also social animals and often ran in packs. I knew this because I was in the midst of reading *Cry of the Kalahari* by Mark and Delia Owens who had spent years in the Kalahari Desert in Botswana documenting the behavior of jackals and lions.

**Namibia Jackal**

Around six we parked on a rise that gave us a panoramic view of the preserve and a great view of the sinking sun. The lodge guide whipped out a folding table, covered it with a tablecloth and on it arranged a variety of wines, gin, and bourbon with mixes. Plus some snacks, chips, peanuts, etc. We once again opted for the drink of choice in these parts—gin and tonic with that powerful dose of quinine in the tonic to ward off malaria although there was no malaria in these parts or so it was claimed.

We then sat down on a circle of logs and watched the sinking sun. Tarry and the guide carried on chatting in Afrikaans probably about some inside company business or gossip.

As they continued nonstop, I remarked to Tarry that Yvonne was originally from Holland and could understand quite a bit of Afrikaans. At that point, they apologized and switched into English and continued to B.S. in the local gossip. I began to realize that the safari community in Namibia was a very small community and that everyone knew everyone and that the local gossip was the coin of the realm.

We watched the final sunset that set off a majestic glow of gold and pink and then we climbed back aboard the Safari truck, happily buzzed and returned to the lodge.

Africa: Around the Edges

**Namibia Sunset**

A word here about the personnel of the lodge. Overall, the staff was friendly and efficient but the female manager was something else. Upon our arrival, she gave us a short welcoming speech in a most perfunctory manner. It was like a parrot talking. Tarry, embarrassed, later remarked that she was new to the job and implied not very good at it. Also at dinner, we discovered that alcoholic drinks were not included. Say what! Karen had said drinks would indeed be included throughout. Nonetheless, we still enjoyed a good bottle of South African Chenin Blanc. Tarry straightened out the drink situation at the end of our stay and offered a refund which I declined saying make it a tip for the staff.

Before we move on, I should digress on the custom of tipping on these safari treks. When I asked the manager back at the Chobe Lodge what was considered customary for tipping the staff, I got a vague answer, basically saying "whatever you feel like." Then I asked what should I tip for the driver/safari guides? Again the same vague answer, "That's personal, between you and him."

She did admit that U.S. dollars and their equivalent in South African Rands would be best. The Aussies at the Chobe camp were pissed that they had to tip at all because in Australia a 10-percent surcharge is automatically placed on every service. The same goes for the European tourist who is used to having a ten percent service charge included. Europeans are very nervous about paying nebulous tip amounts based on personal relationships.

Eventually, I decided to go with the guidelines provided by our travel agent Karen which meant about fifteen to twenty dollars a day per couple to be split up among the camp staff. After consultation with us, the British couple at Hwange did the same. Of course, the big Kahuna in the tipping hierarchy was the driver/guide. Here Cockburn recommended at least fifteen U.S. dollars a day per person for the guides. I later concurred with this because the guides were invaluable with their expertise and keen eyesight as well as their driving abilities. Therefore, a couple of days of touring in the parks would result approximately in about $ 90.00 U.S. tip for the driver between the three of us. I paid this in Rands in Chobe and in U.S. dollars in Hwang since that was the adopted currency.

The rationale behind all this tipping was that the staff and even the guides did not make a very great base pay and had to rely on tips to make ends meet. One could argue that since a family of three on safari for two weeks was spending the equivalent of the price of a modest new car, the last thing one wants to find out is the need for at least seven hundred dollars more to set aside for tipping. Still, it should also be noted that Americans are considered the most generous tippers. Nevertheless, I think tipping guidelines should be much more rigid and fully stated. Even better, put down a known surcharge on the services of the staff and the driver/guides.

***

During our two night stay at the Onguma lodge outside Etosha, I noticed that most of the guests were German. Very snooty, middle-aged Germans. They made it a point to ignore us and never dined with us. I generally like Germans and most young Germans are friendly with Americans as we had experienced at Chobe but here I sensed that these Germans thought us intruders in their own private kingdom.

If you know the history of Namibia, you would know that Germany ran Namibia from the 1880s to their loss of it in World War I in 1918 whereupon, the Brits took over. However, the Germans here acted as if they still owned the place and German influence was everywhere in Namibia from the architecture in the various towns, neat and orderly, to the large expatriate population in the country. Also, there were cheap, direct flights from Dusseldorf to Windhoek, making Namibia especially popular in the winter when it is sunny and warm down here and ass-freezing cold in the fatherland. In short, it is a cheap winter getaway for the Germans.

After dinner, we turned in early because tomorrow it was to be an all-day tour of Etosha National Wildlife Park on an even grander scale than Hwange. Over and out.

# 8. ETOSHA

**Thur. May 3**

You have to understand that Etosha National Wildlife Park is huge. Over 22,000 square kilometers, almost twice the size of Belgium. Not only is it the largest game park in Southern Africa, but it is also perhaps the most iconic in terms of landscape with its great white salt pan, (7,000 square km) and far vistas of bush dotted with acacia trees. Etosha is usually photographed in tourist posters as being the quintessential African wildlife park. It was into this that we would be driving, hoping to see only a small part of it.

**Iconic Etosha**

Thus it was that we were up out and early for our all-day drive. First, we had to stop at the main entrance to the park and check-in with the park rangers.

**Main Gate**

With clipboards in hand, they duly jotted down the license plate number of the vehicle we were in and then collect the park fee for the day. This process involved a few seconds of chit-chat in some tribal language between Tarry and the ranger, probably the latest intelligence on what wildlife was where and other gossip. Then a big smile, the ranger waved us on in.

We drove along for about fifteen minutes on a well-paved road, followed by a few self-drive cars until we came upon a "tower" (i.e. herd) of giraffes strolling along in their graceful, slow-motion but stilt-legged gait that was especially awkward when bending down to drink at a waterhole.

**Awkward**

Of course, zebras were everywhere. These crazy striped horse-like animals had it made as far as I was concerned. Tarry told us they were useless as beasts of burden because their shoulder muscles were too weak to carry a load, let alone a rider. Furthermore, unlike domestic horses, they were unbreakable and therefore unrideable. Still, I remembered how cool it was looking at my Tarzan comic books in the early 50s and seeing Tarzan or Jane riding a zebra. Of course, it was all comic book fiction. As a footnote, they were also tough to eat as well as generally being illegal to hunt.

**Playboys**

Other than fending off a lion now and then with their lethal kicks, Zebras had a good time zipping around the veldt, pausing at waterholes and breeding. Playboys of the savannah. Of course, there was the question of their black and white op-art design. Each set of stripes were unique to each zebra. If you gazed at the patterns too long, it could make you dizzy. Some likened it to fingerprints. I asked Tarry the fundamental question: "Is a Zebra white with black stripes or black with white stripes?"

He said somewhat authoritatively that, "According to the latest research, the zebra's background color is black and that the white stripes and white bellies are additions."

O.K. Duly noted. Black with white stripes. Mystery solved. Moving on we saw a variety of colorful birds flying around and perched in various trees. Tarry paused to point them out to us and snapped some photos. All were unique to Southern Africa.

**Etosha Bird**

As previously mentioned, Tarry had led bird spotting expeditions for bird watchers. He said that while he liked birds, especially for photography, he didn't much care for bird-watcher safaris. He said the birders often drove him nuts, nagging him to stop here and there to photograph very common birds and bitching if they didn't see the rare species listed in their bird books.

We assured him that we enjoyed seeing exotic birds as well and didn't mind him stopping to point out the more unique ones but it was not a priority with us. He seemed relieved. In fact, after a couple of days with Tarry, he was starting to feel like family. After all, he was opening up revealing his pet peeves with us about other Safari clientele, the red tape bureaucracy of the Namibia government and general logistical headaches of running Ultimate Safaris. Also, he and Vanessa appeared to be getting along together in the front seat discussing various TV programs they watched such as the Big Bang Theory. Even though they were ten years apart in age, they seemed of like minds.

After driving around some more and passing by herds of wildebeests, kudus and impalas, we were starting to wonder where the big cats were, namely the lions. Tarry simply shrugged, saying that most of them were probably lying around under acacia trees out of sight, taking it easy. Usually they came out to the waterholes late afternoon and there we would probably see some. Still, I was dubious about a lion sighting because of the lack of lion sightings in Hwange even in the late afternoon. I was more than ever grateful that we had had two great sightings of lions in the Chobe Wildlife Park.

But hark, another safari vehicle drove up and signaled Tarry to stop. He and the other driver/guide had a brief confab in Afrikaans. Then Tarry suddenly drove off at a pace. He turned down a bumpy side dirt road and a hundred yards or so on, he stopped and pointed off into the bush about thirty yards from the road. There it was, a cheetah lying in wait in the grass near a small tree. She wasn't doing much, just waiting perhaps for her main chance at a group of small springboks at a waterhole on the other side of the road. Tarry with his sharp eyes noticed some rustling in the grass near her and using his camera's zoom lens, he focused on a couple of cubs. I used my binoculars but could barely make them out but they were there. Vanessa and Yvonne did the same. Then Tarry and Vanessa clicked away.

**Cheetah**

A note here about Tarry's zoom lens which we had dubbed the "Hubble." It was a humongous lens about 18-inches in length and heavy. Tarry had to grasp a special handle on the lens casing to hold it up. Very cumbersome, I thought as I videoed away with my light little video camera but later, when I saw some of Tarry's pics, I was blown away. His zoom lens put you right in front of the cheetah just inches away. You had the feeling you could reach out and touch her.

We watched for a while and then moved on, skirting the edge of the famous Etosha Pan in the center of the park. We could not drive out on it but merely gaze over its flat, distant, salt white terrain.

**Salt Pan**

What is a "pan," you ask? Well, we asked Tarry and with his encyclopedic knowledge, he informed us that, a pan is a lake bed in a depression that is dry most of the year. The one in Etosha is said to be over a million years old and is 120 kilometers long (75 miles.) After a heavy rain, this pan will be covered with a thin layer of water which is heavily salted but it still supports minimal vegetation for food.

Vulnerable African wildlife like to graze upon the pan or near it in part because by standing on the pan they have a wide field of vision. In other words, they can spot predators a long way off. As we were to discover, all the safari guides were crazy about pans too mainly because you could spot all kinds of wildlife gathered there especially in the wet season. We were at the end of the wet season. Still, it was obvious that you needed high powered binoculars to view the distant wildlife.

Around one, we rolled into a rest spot in a grove of large acacia trees. This to have a picnic lunch and to "stretch our legs." Now this rest spot happened to have lavatory facilities but as mentioned earlier a rest spot often offered nothing but the bush.

Lunch was served with great flair by Tarry. First out was a folding table, then a tablecloth, then silverware, then an assortment of dishes in plastic containers along with various drinks, mostly pop and beer. No sandwiches here. Instead of chicken salad, maybe a pasta salad, coleslaw, sometimes cold bbq chicken. Usually, we had to share our spot with other clients from other guides and all would compare notes with hints of one-upmanship. I found all of this conversation boring and retreated to our van for reading and a short snooze.

After an hour or so of hanging out at this rest spot, we saddled up and headed out again. But, as far as I was concerned, all this wildlife viewing was getting redundant and boring. In addition, riding around all the time and not walking around was getting tiresome. I think Vanessa and Yvonne were getting tired too but just as I was about to tell Tarry to head back to the lodge, he got a call on his radio from a fellow guide saying that the cheetah everyone saw earlier had made a kill and was now visible chowing down on a springbok. So with a shot of adrenaline, we were off back to the area where we first spotted the cheetah.

When we arrived, there were already several trucks and a few self-drives on hand. And lo, there was the beast off about thirty yards feeding on the springbok. He was now standing long and lean, proudly hovering over her kill. We saw most of this up close in binoculars or through zoom lenses. We could also spot her three cubs dancing around, waiting for their turn at the half mutilated carcass.

I sensed that this would be the highlight of the day and urged Tarry to return to the lodge. He protested saying that he wanted to go along a backroad he knew that was sure to have elephants. Elephants were, in fact, one of the major attractions of Etosha. He said this was a must-see and I reluctantly agreed.

Sure enough, after fifteen minutes of bumping along a poor track, we came upon a nicely situated waterhole surrounded by trees. And there in the middle of it was a herd of elephants, about fifteen to twenty of them with babies.

Immediately I was on guard, the memory of pissed-off elephants still fresh in my mind from Hwange. But this group was peaceful and not going anywhere. They were just drinking, foraging and fooling around spraying each other with their spouts of water from their trunks.

**Bath Time**

All was well for a while, then suddenly out of bush came a big bull elephant charging towards the main bull elephant of the herd. This was a real beast running along and looking very scary. Tons of elephant meat on the hoof thundering along. Immediately, most of the herd formed a circle to protect their young, while the main bull elephant of the herd charged towards the bigger bull.

What followed next was a spectacular fight between the two bull elephants. They butted heads and then tried to gore each other with their tusks, stomping around all the while. This went on for several minutes before the challenging bull figured he had had enough and broke off the battle.

*Africa: Around the Edges*

**Charging Bulls**

Tarry pointed out that although larger, the challenger bull was much older and not up to fighting another younger bull in prime condition. Soon our challenger bull was crashing off into the underbrush again. We had witnessed one of the iron laws of nature—survival of the fittest.

That was the capper to our day. We returned forthwith to the lodge, had a round of gin and tonics on the veranda and then retired to our bungalows for a short rest before dinner. Satisfied with the day's outing but still hoping that tomorrow that we would see some lions.

**Fri. May 4**

The next morning, we went out for another full day drive through the park but this time to its southern border. This would be our last day in Etosha. The plan was to exit the park at the Anderson Gate and drive on to another lodge, the Ongava Lodge, about an hour outside of Etosha.

As we drove along stopping here and there, Tarry pointed out various birds and fauna. We were alone out here in this area of the park but as we skirted a waterhole, we spotted two large rhinos grazing peacefully about 20-yards off the road. Both were monsters sporting lethal-looking horns, obvious prizes for poachers. These rhinos were not at all threatening.

**Full Horn Rhinos**

They simply stood there grazing, ignoring us. Tarry said they couldn't see us because their eyesight was so bad but they could hear us so no sharp sounds. Luckily for the moment, we were the only ones observing them and of course, photographing them. Then about five minutes later a couple of other safari trucks rolled up, making a lot of noise. We decided not to stick around and moved on.

A few minutes later we drove by a herd of Hartebeests also with the magnificent corkscrew horns and a herd of Oryx with less spectacular horns.

*Africa: Around the Edges*

**Hartebeest**

Then all at once Tarry stopped the truck, raised the roof and with his Hubble-like lens proceeded to take photos of two beautiful cranes, silver blue, sleek and only a few yards off in the bush. Tarry said the Blue Crane was an endangered bird. We sat for a while feasting on their visual beauty as they strutted around pecking the ground not noticing us at all.

**Blue Crane**

Along the way, we ran into across scores of jackals, my favorite scavenger as noted earlier. They are always so busy scouting around, searching for food for themselves and their offspring. They can live on anything and often the jackal is the only wild creature surviving in a harsh desert environment especially during a drought when all the other wildlife has fled or simply died off.

**Day of the Jackal**

We took a brief rest stop for a mid-morning snack. Already we were thinking of lunch but Tarry said lunch would be late because he wanted to take us to the best rest stop in the park, the Okaukuejo Rest Camp. "It's a real resort. You can sit down to a served lunch and even take a swim if you want."

O.K. I guess we will starve until then.

It was a good thing that we didn't pause for a longer break because Tarry got an urgent call on his van radio. A leopard had been spotted up in a tree near a certain waterhole. The caller urged him to get over there quick because other vehicles were pouring in.

So the race was on. Tarry gunned the safari wagon and we flew over a secondary dirt road, arriving ten minutes later at the tree and waterhole in question. Tarry managed to squeeze by several other vehicles so we had a great view of the tree with the leopard. Except when we looked at the tree only fifty feet off, we saw no leopard.

Tarry looking through his telephoto lens, said "Yes, I see him there well camouflaged what with his spots. He is wrapped around the branches."

I looked through my binoculars and managed to make the leopard out. From what I could see he was a long, powerful bugger even though obscured by the branches. The leopard was stone-still, like a statue. His head was turned away from us presumably staring down a herd of springboks at the nearby waterhole waiting for his main chance.

We sat and watched this statue for a good ten minutes. It was actually getting boring, and then the leopard turned his head towards us to check us out. At that moment Tarry and Vanessa snapped photos like crazy. The leopard then turned back towards his intended prey.

**Leopard in a Tree**

It now became a traffic jam around this site with scores of self-drives showing up along with several more safari vans. Finally, Tarry said enough, "We got to get out of here before we are blocked in."

Even so, Tarry had to drive off into the bush to get around the mess. As far as we could tell, the leopard ignored it all and concentrated on his prey.

Following our encounter with the leopard in the tree, we hustled over to the nearby Okaukuejo Rest Camp, our stomachs growling. I had expected nothing more than a snack stand and an outhouse (if we were lucky.) But lo, this was indeed a spread. The grounds were extensive with cabins for hire. There were also camping and RV areas on the grounds. There was a large crystalline pool that was very inviting with a bunch of kids running around.

**Okaukuejo Rest Camp**

Best of all, there was a full-service restaurant serving a buffet lunch. You could also order a burger at a nearby snack stand. I opted for the buffet lunch but was careful about what I chose since I was getting worried about gaining weight. Seemed like all we had done on this trip was eat and drink (alcohol) and ride around to our heart's content. Hardly any exercise at all.

We dined under an outdoor veranda. It was all very mellow, the weather perfect, somewhere in the mid-70s. Tarry kept exclaiming how green everything was. Again, I didn't think the countryside was that green but apparently compared to its normal state, the veldt was considered green. Finally, lunch over, I walked around the grounds videoing this and that. Then we bought ice cream cones and were on our way again, this time out of the park

\*\*\*

*Africa: Around the Edges*

O.K. so that was the last of Etosha. We were only slightly disappointed that we had not seen any lions but apparently they didn't get the memo to show up. Tarry insisted they were there in spades. I told him we believed him but since we had already seen lions in Chobe, it was no big deal. Still, I was intrigued by the lack of lions in a general way. I had heard that limited lion hunting was allowed in Namibia and that if a lion strayed from a protected national park-like Etosha onto cattle grazing land, it could be hunted and shot. Tarry said that was indeed true. "Can't have lions killing off cattle. Beef is a big export product here," was the common refrain.

Further, according to Tarry, there were several private game preserves in Namibia where if you were willing to pay a lot of money, you could hunt lions. All of this was legal if limited in Namibia unlike Botswana which allowed no big game hunting at all.

This comported with what I had read earlier about Namibia. The standard rationale behind big game hunting in Namibia including for lions and other prime game was that the revenue it generated helped pay for the conservation efforts of wildlife and led to the employment of hundreds of Namibians. In addition, according to statistics, the number of wildlife critters killed by hunters was minuscule compared to the extent of herds which abounded in Namibia and in no way threatened their existence. In fact, the greatest threat to wildlife everywhere in Africa was the expansion of the human population and the battle over scarce agriculture resources. Another major threat to wildlife far more than legal hunting was the poachers going after prime species such as black rhinos and elephants.

***

While we are on the subject let's jump ahead a bit. On our flight back to the states, we encountered a group of Texans and Utahans who had just completed a big game hunting safari in South Africa. They were a burly, loud bunch bragging about their kills. We sat next to one of them, Hank, who was a little less boisterous and seemed like a reasonable fellow. At first, he was a little defensive when we inquired about his big game hunting experience. But as we talked and he realized that I was not totally against big game hunting in general, he opened up, explaining that most of the kills on the private preserve where he hunted were the kudu with their fantastic spiral horns.

The conversation went like this:

**Me:** Well there are certainly plenty of kudus around.

**Hank:** Yeah, there are and you know they are pretty easy to hunt. I almost felt like I was cheating.

**Me:** What about lions and elephants?

**Hank:** Oh No. They are off-limits and anyway, we didn't have a license to hunt for those.

**Me:** Yeah, I guess hunting lions and elephants is expensive. Only for the rich like the Trump kids. By the way, did you see that photo of that Donald Jr. and Erick Trump posing with their lion kill?

**Hank:** Yeah, I saw that but no, I am content. I got a beautiful kudu with probably with the biggest spiral horns of the group.

**Me:** So are you going to stuff it and take it back to the states?

**Hank:** Oh, no. Not all of it. Just the head and horns. The rest of the kudu went for meat locally. It helps feed the villagers.

**Me:** So you think that you are doing some good here?

**Hank:** Yeah, I think so. We got our trophies and villagers got to eat prime kudu. I had some. It tastes great, almost like beef.

**Me:** Yeah, we have been having a lot of kudu ourselves. Who knows? Maybe the kudu meat we ate came from a trophy hunter kill.

**Hank:** Who knows? Maybe.

\*\*\*

As we drove along, this time on paved roads out of the park, I began to wonder about our abode for the night. Karen had told us that the Ongava Lodge was a rather plush place up on a ridge overlooking a game reserve. She didn't say which game reserve. I had assumed it would be the Etosha game reserve.

As an hour went by, some of it now on extremely rough gravel roads, I was beginning to wonder where the fuck Ongava Lodge was. It was certainly far from Etosha Park proper. When we finally arrived at the Ongava Lodge around four, it was indeed a very plush lodge situated on a hill with a big view of a preserve, their own private preserve.

**Ongava Lodge**

A private preserve, you say! Yes! This lodge had an extensive private preserve. I immediately had the impression that all wildlife viewing activities were done in this private preserve, not in Etosha more than an hour away. As far as we were concerned, I thought it didn't make much sense to stay here for only a night after all our game viewing in Etosha. But here we were.

We were greeted by an unusually enthusiastic staff singing and dancing led by the live wire manager called Molly. We were ushered in, handed a fruit drink and registered. Then we were shown to our lodgings which turned out to be rather luxurious suites with no pretense of being a tent like our other lodgings. Simply a good old fashion hotel type suite with a sweeping balcony view of the bush and a nearby waterhole.

**Our Room**

After we settled in, Yvonne and Vanessa went off for a swim at the main lodge while I chilled. Early evening before the others, I went over to the main lodge for a gin and tonic sundowner on the patio and there was Tarry with another guide from Unlimited Safaris discussing business in Afrikaans.

I sat there soaking up the atmosphere, overhearing some lady from South Africa at the next table relate the latest news about a murder of a farm family in South Africa and the murder of a tourist family in Angola. I thought to myself, what an alarmist! Also, why would a tourist go to Angola which had a murderous reputation for anyone, tourist or local alike? This I remembered from Paul Theroux's *Last Train to Zona Verde*.

By and by, I excused myself to get another drink and ran into a friendly fellow from Texas. We chatted for a while. He said he was from Houston and traveling with his mom instead of his wife who was scared of Africa due to the current news about murders and bribes, etc.

As he explained, "My wife was overreacting but my mom was adamant, she wanted to go on an African safari before she died. Of course, that's a long way off. She's only in her early 70s and she is in excellent health."

Later I spotted a very old lady sitting at the table with the guide that Tarry had been talking to. It was only her and the guide. Tarry later explained that he was escorting this woman in her late 80s around Southern Africa for three weeks and that she was crabby and demanding.

But she was full of spirit saying "Fuck all, I'm going to see Africa before I die."

I felt sorry for the guide at having to put up with that and still be pleasant. As Tarry said, that was the name of the game. You couldn't help but be sympathetic to someone on what was a once-in-a-lifetime trip and who was probably going to die soon anyway.

By this time Yvonne and Vanessa had arrived for dinner and we dug in. Once again the food was great, although I had a local fish because I was worried about calories. So did Vanessa. Yvonne and Tarry had a slab of kudu which they proclaimed the best yet. I ordered a bottle of Chenin Blanc to go with the fish for Vanessa and me while the others had a couple of glasses of red wine.

As we sipped on our wine, we fully realized that we were at the end of our time on a wildlife safari in Africa. We had seen almost every species of wildlife, some of it in very dramatic circumstances. Except we had not seen any hyenas. It would have been nice to have seen at least one hyena. Tarry said you usually found them if you go out at night and that we might run into some down in the desert after dark. We would see. In any case tomorrow it was on to Swakopmund, the jumping-off spot to the Skeleton Coast and the famous sand dunes of Sossusvlei.

# 9. SWAKOPMUND

**Sat. May 5**

It was only 500 kilometers (310 miles) but our early morning drive to Swakopmund from our hotel took almost six hours, much of it over gravel roads. Much of the drive was long, hot and boring. Thank god for our air-conditioned safari truck with comfortable leather seats and good shock absorbers. Oh, there were frequent stops along the way. Stops for snacks, diesel, tourist trinkets and bathroom breaks. Still, it was an ordeal. A lot of the countryside was monotonous, flat with low scrub brush, much similar to where we lived in Colorado on a high desert plateau but with no scenic mountains in the background.

However, when we hit a series of towns, our interest was piqued. To wit, Outjo was a charming gateway village to Etosha. Neat as a pin and rather prosperous looking. Farther on we came to Otjiwarongo, a rather large commercial town with busy people on Saturday errands. Next, we drove through Omaruru which was a farming and dairy center and finally Karibib, the center of marble mining in Namibia.

I expressed surprise that Namibia had marble quarries. "But of course, Mein Herr." intoned Tarry. He explained that in fact, much of the marble, mainly white marble, was exported worldwide came from Namibia. "It's cheaper than Italian marble and is of the same quality," he continued. Indeed as we passed by several marble quarries, to my untrained eye, from a distance, the marble did look impressive.

**Marble Quarry**

In short, thanks to mining, farming and tourism, all these Namibia towns looked prosperous and peaceful with none of the tacky slums said to surround many towns in Southern Africa. To further add to the impression of prosperity, many of the local Namibians we saw about appeared well dressed and drove late-model cars.

However, I knew from my reading that up north on the border of Namibia and Angola, it was a lot poorer than the rest of the country, especially for the San people who were ancestors of the ancient hunter-gatherers that roamed this country for thousands of years. Paul Theroux and others have written about them, how dirt poor they were, how disease-prone they were and how they had been driven off their ancestral lands. Claiming that the Namibian government does little for them despite official protest to the contrary. Unfortunately, we were never going to see any of these people. We were sticking to the approved upscale tourist route.

***

Coming out of Karibib, we turned off and headed west on the main route to Swakopmund about 169 kilometers away. After an hour or so, the terrain turned into a deep, sandy desert with low cactus type bushes. We passed by several large-scale mining operations for various minerals including uranium. According to Tarry many of these operations were owned and run by the Chinese, a fact which didn't seem to bother him.

Soon we were nearing Swakopmund and as we did so, the name kept running through my mind. Swakopmund? Swakopmund? Who would ever name a town that? Especially Germans? It sounded "Swakop-wacky" to me.

Later I looked up the derivation of the name. Actually, the name Swakopmund is a combination of two words. "Swakop" is a tribal word that means an opening and is the name of the river that flows to the sea through the town. "Mund" is a German word that means mouth. So together, the town is named after the mouth of the Swakop River. Now the less charitable would remind you that "Swakop" also means excrement or shit. Thus, the town can be referred to as the "asshole" of the Namibia coast.

However, when entered the town what we saw was a nice, tidy community with hints of German-style architecture.

**Swakopmund**

Since it was only three-thirty, Tarry gave us a quick drive around town. Aside from its vaguely German look, Swakopmund was a thriving tourist center with many busy shops and a lot of young people about. Tarry said it was now an "in" place for the young, especially for backpacking Europeans. They came to this end-of-the-world place on the Atlantic coast for hang-gliding, windsurfing, dune buggy riding and sandboarding on the dunes. They often ignored the game parks in Namibia but there were spectacular nature tours here, as well. All of this happened on the beaches just north of town in the Dorob National Park. Further south were the beaches of the infamous Skeleton Coast our destination for the next day.

As we drove around, Yvonne spotted a shop that focused on authentic African art and artifacts. She had read about it in Fodor's Guide. It was famous in Namibia—Peter's Antiques.

**Peter's Antiques**

This being Saturday, Yvonne was sure it was open and indeed it was. We parked and she and I entered this establishment chock full of artifacts such as African masks, weapon-like axes, spears, various fetishes, and fertility statues. On the second floor was a stash of Nazi paraphernalia that was popular with both Germans and non-Germans alike.

**Artifacts**

Tarry and Vanessa wandered off in different directions while Yvonne and I took a look at the offerings. The shop was run by a cranky old German lady who barely spoke English but her collection was vast. All prices fixed, no bargaining. We went immediately to the tribal room where Yvonne examined the masks and other artifacts. They did look authentic. Defiantly not for the tourist trade, also expensive but after a few minutes of looking around I got bored, plus I was thirsty. I excused myself from the premises, telling Yvonne not to spend more than two hundred bucks on anything. Her response was, "Hey, you still owe me for a couple of birthdays."

O.K., O.K.

I repaired to the bar next door and sat outside under an awning joining Tarry who was already there enjoying a beer. I ordered a round of gin and tonics because Vanessa who had been photographing the town soon showed up. So we drank and chilled, admiring the tidy and picturesque town of Swakopmund.

Soon Yvonne came out from the shop with her prize, a spectacular African fertility statue and joined us. By and by, Tarry announced that we should check in to the guesthouse where we were staying and then later, we would go out to his favorite fish restaurant, the Tug.

"Wait till you see it. An entire restaurant housed in an old tugboat. The fish is great too," he boasted.

We then drove over to our lodging for the night, the Cornerstone Guest House on the edge of town not too far from the ocean. This was a neat looking establishment, modest but comfortable and certainly adequate for a night's stay. As we discovered it was run by a couple of German women. The guests were mostly German too but young Germans touring Africa on the cheap. Very friendly, not like the old dodgy Germans we had encountered at Etosha.

We rested up for a while and then around 6:30, Tarry gathered us up for dinner at the Tug. We drove over to the main waterfront area and there it was, an industrial size tugboat permanently beached with buildouts for part of the restaurant. This was the tugboat that once towed huge tankers and container ships.

**The Tug**

We entered its portals, climbed the stairs to the main deck and came out upon a lively restaurant and bar scene decorated with all kinds of nautical bric-a-brac. The joint was jumping with young and old drinking large steins of what I assumed were German beer and Afro-pop music in the background. I did notice that most of the patrons were white tourists and white locals with a scattering of Africans. Tarry had reserved a prime table for us on the main deck and soon we were feasting on lobster, bream and other assorted fish and chips dishes washed down with good German beer.

While we were dining, a couple of attractive blonde girls in their twenties came up and said hello to Tarry and chatted in German. They were local Germans born and raised in Namibia and seemed very friendly. As much as I could make out since my German was minimal, they were encouraging Tarry to join them at some party or get together later that evening. Tarry seemed receptive. I began to wonder just how faithful our fiancéed Tarry really was to his girlfriend. Even Vanessa later remarked on this. She confided that she thought Tarry was a player when it came to women. "Well, that's life," I said, remembering an old French saying "When love is distant, it often fades." Or at least is put on hold for a while.

After dinner, Yvonne and I walked around on the beachfront out back for a while, mesmerized by the crashing surf. It was hypnotic. That was the only thing missing on this trip so far, the crashing ocean and smell of sea salt. Vanessa and Tarry had returned to the van and waited patiently for us. Later, we took group pictures of each other.

**Tarry & Vanessa**

*Africa: Around the Edges*

**The Browns**

Afterward, Tarry dropped us off at the guest house saying he had to go meet some friends. He would see us tomorrow for our next big day in Namibia.

# 10. SOSSUSVLEI

**Sun. May 6**

The next morning Tarry showed up bright and chipper. I guess he hadn't partied that hard. Tarry was not chauffeuring us today because we were flying on a charter flight down the Skeleton Coast to the Namibia dune area of Sossusvlei. Tarry would be driving our luggage down there because the charter plane could not take the extra weight. I had thought that this would take Tarry a good part of the day but he insisted he could do it in three hours and therefore, he was going to chill this morning for a while before he left.

As explained before this charter flight was an extra expense that we were encouraged to take by Karen because it was supposed to offer spectacular views of the Atlantic coastline in a very remote area. Additionally, we were supposed to fly low over the remains of old shipwrecks and a diamond mining camp. Finally, we would get a bird's eye view of the dunes of Sossusvlei before landing near our lodge for the night. All of this for five hundred dollars extra per person. Would it be worth it?

Perhaps a bit of background here. The Skeleton Coast is called that because it was a navigational nightmare for 18$^{th}$ and 19$^{th}$-century vessels, indeed even for vessels from the 16$^{th}$-century Portuguese era. It is a coast of storms and deadly Atlantic crosscurrents in frigid waters. The coast is said to be littered with shipwrecks, bleached whale bones and even human bones.

Further, the Skeleton Coast backs up to miles and miles of desert sand dunes. Human habitation is scarce. If you are going to penetrate it by land you need a four-wheel-drive vehicle with a winch and plenty of supplies and extra gas to navigate even a small portion of its non-existent roads. The only way to see a good part of the Skeleton Coast within a few hours was, of course, to fly over it.

Around nine, a representative from Scenic Air Charter Services arrived at our guesthouse to drive us over the airport for our flight. After a short drive, he dropped us off at the small terminal and hurried off. The terminal was deserted except for a clerk slouched over a desk snoozing away. Not a very active place at this hour it seemed.

Vanessa and I looked out the back of the terminal building and saw a couple of pilot types on the tarmac preparing a small Cessna aircraft for flight. I judged that this was to be our plane. Small.

**Our Plane**

We returned to the terminal and sat down in a waiting area with Vanessa looking visibly upset.

| | |
|---|---|
| **Her**: | You know I get airsick don't you? |
| **Me**: | No, I didn't know that. |
| **Her**: | I'll be lucky if I don't throw up. |
| **Me**: | Take one of those pills for seasickness. |
| **Her**: | I already did but I don't know if it will work. Plus the plane is so small, I might get claustrophobia. |
| **Me**: | Swell, then maybe you should have gone with Tarry in the Safari vehicle. |
| **Her**: | I don't know. I guess I will be alright. |

She slouched back in her seat, resigned.

About this time, the pilot, a slim, blond-haired fellow, showed up. He introduced himself as Phil and began briefing us on what we would be seeing by pointing out locations and photos on a map. He was a rather young looking but he seemed to know his stuff.

**Skeleton Coast Map**

His briefing: "It will be about an hour flight down the coast and to our destination in Sossusvlei. Along the way, we should see some amazing things. First up will be Wallis Bay, a major industrial port just down the coast from Swakopmund. Usually, it's full of tankers and containers from around the world. This port has been of strategic importance for the southwest coast of Africa since its discovery during the time of the Portuguese. Known for its fishing and whaling, for most of its history, this portion of the Atlantic coast has been controlled mostly by the Dutch and the British. It was permanently handed over to Namibia in 1994; four years after Namibia became independent.

"Next we will see miles and miles of stunning coastline, often surrounded by dunes coming right up to the water's edge. Then there are the remains of a German cargo ship grounded in 1907. Following that, we will fly over an old diamond mining camp, the remnants of which you can still make out today. Finally, we will do a short sightseeing flight over the dunes of Sossusvlei. And then we land at the Sossusvlei Lodge airport. That'll be it. Any questions?'"

He looked around. Nothing from us although I privately thought he was offering a lot for an hour flight.

"No questions. O.K. let's go."

Phil led us out to the Cessna and deposited Yvonne and Vanessa in the cramped backseat and me because of my size and weight in the cramped front, co-pilot seat. Fine by me. He claimed that the views would be great wherever we were seated.

He then went through a flight checklist, started the single-engine and soon we were rolling down the runway of the little airport. A few seconds later we were airborne soaring over the town. The views were already magnificent with the cobalt blue ocean on one side, the town and the desert beyond on the other.

In a matter of minutes, we were flying over Wallis Bay, only a few miles south of Swakopmund. Indeed the bay and harbor were impressive. It was a horseshoe-shaped bay with a radius of several miles filled with extensive docking facilities. Today, however, ships were scarce and those which were around in the bay looked lonely.

**Wallis Bay**

Flying on, we soon entered the remote part of the Skeleton Coast. Looking down, all we could see were miles and miles of surf splashing up onto wide beaches and in some cases up onto dunes which came right down to the seashore.

**Skeleton Coast**

The most amazing part was that beaches such as these would be full of people in the U.S. Here they were virtually deserted. We didn't see any vehicle or camp down there. Of course, it should be remembered that these waters were cold with temperatures in the 50s and full of sharks and deadly rip currents. Not at all inviting to swimmers or surfer or boaters in general.

After about twenty minutes in the air, we came to our first major sighting of a shipwreck, the Eduard Bohlen, a German cargo ship that went aground in 1907.

**German Cargo Ship**

Later we passed over the diamond mine camp but all we saw were faint outlines of the foundations of the worn away structures. Admittedly, even at a lower altitude, there would not be much more to see of this camp. Still, it was annoying that the Phil appeared to be blowing off this sightseeing portion of the flight by staying at altitude and not circling around points of interest. Was he in a hurry to get to a hot date or what? However, we were so clueless and sensing our lives were in this guy's hands, we didn't think to ask him to fly at a lower sightseeing altitude.

The best part of the flight came near the end when we entered the Sossusvlei dune area and had a bird's eye view of row after row of gigantic dunes rising up from the desert floor like mighty centennials. These dunes were truly impressive and gave lie to my notion that once you had seen one large dune, you had seen them all.

**Sossusvlei dunes**

A mere ninety minutes' drive from where we live in Colorado, we have the Great Sand Dunes National Park which has some impressive dunes itself but nothing like this. Sadly, this aerial tour of the dunes came to an end all too soon as we approached our destination airfield.

**Cockpit**

Down, down we went but when we came within feet of touching down Phil pulled up as if he had missed the runway and circled around, coming down again, this time seemingly inches off the ground, except we weren't over the runway. We were over a field of gravel that preceded the runway and the plane's sirens were going off, signaling an engine stall was imminent. We had to land right then and it looked as if we were going to land on the gravel. But not quite. We managed to make it to the beginning of the concrete runway but when the Cessna finally touched down, it did so on one wheel and with a large thud as the other wheel came crashing down, knocking us about. Then nothing. Silence. We were down.

We were in one piece and not tipped over as I had envisioned. We taxied over to the hanger with Phil apologizing for the rough landing. I diplomatically mentioned that there must have been a crosswind to throw things off. He nodded and didn't dispute me. Actually, based on my own limited experience in small plane landings, this was a fucked-up landing with the pilot solely responsible. Phil was very quiet as he led us off the plane and into the small terminal where a ride was awaiting us to take us to our hotel.

Later thinking this over, I had to conclude that this particular charter flight was probably not worth the money. I mean the seashore was scenic but not exceptional from the air. I had seen much the same along the northern California coastline from the air. The so-called wreaks and relics were minor. Only the dunes were spectacular and these could have been viewed from the air by hot air balloon. Karen had mentioned that balloon flights were four hundred per person and much more relaxing than a fixed-wing flight. Something to keep in mind for the next time, if indeed there was to be a next time.

Oh, yes, I later heard from Tarry when I complained about our flight was that Phil had been rushed in this flight because he had a return charter with passengers waiting for him and he was behind schedule.

No kidding. Anyway as we were being driven over to our hotel, the Hoodia Desert Lodge, we passed Tarry going the other way in his safari wagon. He spotted us, honked and turned around, whereupon we stopped dismounted from our van and climbed into his.

I remarked that he had made good time getting down here in only a couple of hours or so. Tarry said it was nothing. He had taken some shortcuts that he knew and sped down here over bumpy gravel roads but with no passengers to complain about it, (ha-ha,) he could go like a bear.

It was about a twenty-minute ride to Hoodia Desert Lodge (a strange almost voodoo-like name) but when we arrived there we could see it was a class establishment butted up against a range of craggy hills. This time no singing staff which was a relief. Just a hyperactive manager with an East European accent and an old buddy of Tarry based on their hugs.

The staff took off with our luggage while we retired to the lounge/lobby and a round of complimentary welcome drinks, this time with alcohol. The lounge/lobby area was vast, well-appointed with leather couches and easy chairs and tables full of nature magazines, books and chessboards sets.

Off to the side, two large world globes were turned to an accurate scale depiction of Africa which you could see that next to greater Asia was the second largest continent on the planet. Usually on a Mercator projected flat map, Africa is depicted as being much smaller. Africans claim that's because the colonial powers who drew the maps were racists in their depiction of Africa as only a minor continent on the world's stage.

**Hoodia Desert Lodge**

Following the meet and greet, we were escorted to our rooms, once again in the African bungalow mode, but hopefully devoid of wildlife intrusion. Yvonne went down for a nap while I suited up for a swim in their crystalline pool next to the main lodge. So far this trip I had not gone swimming. After padding over there with my swim mask and hotel provided bathrobe, I plunged into the crystal waters and immediately jumped right out. It was ice cold. How could it be so cold here in the desert with the hot desert sun? " Chicken," I told myself and after a few seconds eased myself back into the pool, slowly getting used to the cold water. Soon, I was numb to the cold and happily splashing around and swimming laps. After twenty minutes of this, I got out and lounged in the still warm sun. I also had a great view of the craggy hills out back of the hotel. I guess we were indeed in the much hallowed Namibian desert. Tomorrow the dunes.

# 11. DUNES

**Mon. May 7**

Early the next morning after a light breakfast, we set off for the Sossusvlei dunes around 6 a.m. It was an hour's drive to the dunes area of the park, officially known as the Namib-Naukluft Park. When we arrived at the main entrance, we were already behind a long line of cars and vans. As we crawled along what was in effect a valley of dunes, we looked out on some truly awesome dunes, more impressive from the ground level than from the air. Catching the early morning light, they took on a surreal quality of light and shadow much like a Salvador Dali painting.

**Sossusvlei Dune**

We eventually came to the main parking lot of these monsters but the lot was already filled with scores of dune hikers gearing up and milling around. But ever resourceful Tarry drove to the end of the park and found a hideaway rest spot under a grove of trees well away from the mob.

Further, this spot was strategically placed so that Tarry could satisfy the disparate desires of the Brown family. For instance, it was a short hike to the base of "Big Daddy," the tallest dune in the park at a thousand feet of elevation which Vanessa had vowed to climb. It was a lesser hike to the dune that I wanted to climb, "Little Daddy," which was an arm of Big Daddy but not nearly so high at about 500-feet. Then right in front of us was a gentle little dune walk for Yvonne whose ankle was hurting. This walk would take her to some of the classic pans so often photographed at the foot of the big dunes, pans like Deadviel. Tarry would accompany Yvonne. Vanessa and I were on our own.

**Big Daddy & Little Daddy**

Without missing a beat, Vanessa hustled off on the trail to Big Daddy. With a water bottle in hand, I trekked over to the starting point of my hike up Little Daddy. There I joined a line of middle-aged French tourists hiking up. I couldn't pass them because the trail was so narrow but seeing me hiking along faster than they were going, they motioned that I should lead because I was probably faster. *"Vous EST plus vite!"* they exclaimed. So I went ahead of the group.

The first hundred feet of elevation going up the dune was not bad, not too steep but then the dune rose precipitously and I began navigating a knife-edge path in the loose sand. You had to keep a balance or you could easily slip off the path and down one side or another. No big deal but rather embarrassing in front of the other hikers.

Since I was a big guy, I endeavored to step in the compacted steps of previous hikers going up the dune and that worked pretty well. Of course, the French tourists happily followed in my heavier compacted tracks. But really, dune hiking was not my thing. Often for every step forward, you can slide back two if you were not careful. It's a lot of effort, even though I was in relatively good shape for someone in their 70s. I continued to plow ahead, occasionally pausing to catch my breath and taking in the scenery. I motioned once for the French to go ahead but once again but they said no. They would take a pause too and snap some pictures. They were a funny group. One older one kept asking me where I had learned French. *"En France, bien sur,"* I replied.

During our pause, we had a great view of the valley and the other dunes of which I took video. Finally, I and my little band of Frenchies approached what appeared to be the peak of Little Daddy. As we did so, I saw Tarry bounding his way up the side of the dune taking giant steps in the sand. When he got to the top, he pulled out his camera and started snapping pictures me in my final ascent. Below is a photo of me in the foreground and the Frenchies in the background.

*Africa: Around the Edges*

**Allan on Top**

I congratulated Tarry about his springbok abilities in scaling the dune and then wondered where he had left Yvonne.

"Don't worry. She's fine. We took a little hike to one of the pans with the dead trees on it. She is waiting there sitting on a log. I'll return to her in a minute."

Then Tarry told me he had been tracking Vanessa up to the summit of Big Daddy through his zoom lens. I took a look through the lens and there she was with some Japanese tourists all hovering around the peak. Later she took this photo at the summit.

**Vanessa on Top**

"So, you see. All is good, Allan. Now I'll rejoin Yvonne." With that Tarry bounded down the dune, in giant leaps, half skidding, half surfing it, all the way down, whooping it up as he went. I said what the hell and followed him, taking big leaps and skidding down the sand myself. A couple of times I slipped down in the sand ass-first but got up and kept going. It was almost like sledding.

Whatever it was, it was the quickest way down and before I knew it, I had hit the bottom. I then followed a little trail and soon spotted Yvonne sitting on the log. No sign of Tarry. I wondered where Tarry had gone to. In any case, Yvonne complained that she had been waiting so long and it was getting hot. Remember it was only nine in the morning or so but the sun was starting to beat down already.

Tarry had given Yvonne the van keys so we returned to the van about a quarter-mile off in the shady alcove of trees. There, we drank some cold Gatorade and chilled until Tarry returned. He then started setting up for a picnic breakfast.

By and by, Vanessa showed up, looking tired but inspired. "Boy, that was a climb! Really mind-blowing. Dad, it does put those Colorado dunes to shame. The only problem was all those other tourists on the trail. Many of them, Japanese. They held me back. You really can't pass on that narrow dune trail."

Now seeing the spread that Tarry had laid out, Vanessa cut short her rant and said, "Hey, let's eat."

So we sat down and had ourselves a late breakfast as it was now approaching 10 a.m. After that, we packed up and Tarry took us on a tour of the rest of the national park for a couple of hours, explaining the geology of the area and answering the question of how come there were so many dunes.

As he pointed out, we were in a dune valley about twenty kilometers long. In addition to their fanciful nicknames like Big Daddy, each major dune was numbered in order to keep track of them because they changed position constantly.     Contrary to common belief these dunes were not formed by water or from sand blown in from the Atlantic. Rather they were formed by wind blowing in from central Namibia. Huh? Further, Big Daddy was technically in the area of the park known as Deadviel which referred to the pan at the base. A favorite spot for photographers because of the silhouettes of the dead trees.

**Deadviel**

At one point in our drive, we came across a small Subaru self-drive stuck in the sand. The driver was gunning the engine and spinning out, digging himself even deeper into the sand. Tarry immediately stopped and jumped out to help the guy. He first deflated the four tires a bit and then instructed the driver to slowly engage the gears and move slowly forward and then back. At this point, another guide joined Tarry and together they rocked the car back and forth and slowly it began to get a gripe and finally cleared its sand trap. All of this took a bare five minutes and we were on our way again

I remarked to Tarry that he was such a Good Samaritan. Tarry responded, "It was nothing. It happens all the time with these self-drives. The tourists driving them haven't a clue about driving in sand. It can be treacherous around here. I have to help them though. I have even been stuck myself now and then."

***

Around noon, we drove out of the park and were on our way back to the lodge. Arriving an hour later, we dispersed to our respective bungalows to chill and rest up from our early morning endeavors. Tarry wanted to know if we wanted to go out for a late afternoon drive. We demurred, saying we wanted to rest and get ready for our drive tomorrow back to Windhoek.

"Well let's at least do another sundowner that I owe you."

"Sure."

Around six we went out again and had our last sundowner in Namibia under a baobab tree watching the sun sink behind a range of low lying scrub hills.

Later after dinner when it was dark, I asked Tarry to give us an astronomy lesson about the southern hemisphere. I specifically wanted him to point out the Southern Cross, something that I thought I had seen before in Australia and New Zealand but was never sure about it.

So we all trooped out a bit into the desert and gazed up at the night sky which in the crystalline atmosphere the stars were so pure and ablaze that you felt you could reach out and touch them. Then Tarry, with a laser pointer in hand, proceeded to give us an astronomy lesson about all the southern constellations. First, he pinpointed the Southern Cross which wasn't all that prominent compared to many other stars in the southern night sky. You had to really use your imagination to visualize a cross. I guess its basic importance for navigation was as a guide to true South.

**Southern Cross**

Much easier to figure out in the night sky was the constellation of Scorpio with its whip-like tail. Tarry remarked that while Scorpio was also visible in the northern hemisphere, it was much more prominent and dynamic in the southern hemisphere.

**Scorpio**

Tarry went on to point out a lot more constellations visible primarily in the Southern Hemisphere like he was a professor of astronomy. It was impressive. Our man Tarry, a real Renaissance man of Namibia.

Afterward, we returned to our bungalows and retired for the night. Well not quite. Vanessa talked me into a chess game in the lounge. We played a couple of games but I was tired and couldn't concentrate. At least that was my excuse, as she handily beat me both times.

Tomorrow a long drive back to Windhoek and thence a flight to our last destination on this mad African sojourn—a week in Cape Town.

## 12. WINDHOEK

**Tue. May 8**

Early the next morning we were off to Windhoek. Before we left, Vanessa and I gave Tarry a well-deserved tip for his time with us. Roughly $320.00 US. Taking the folding money and stuffing into his shirt pocket, he didn't even count it but did thank us profusely for the dough. I suspected it was going to be his mad money for his vacation next week to Mozambique with his fiancée.

Our departure was delayed momentarily due to what we thought was a dead battery. Huh? The much-vaunted customized Toyota safari van, had a dead battery? Not to worry though because it had two batteries. However, when Tarry switched over to the other battery, it still didn't start. I began to suspect that it was more than a dead battery, maybe the alternator. When that baby goes out forget it and call the tow truck.

Never mind, quick as a flash one of the staff rolled up in a pickup, hooked up the leads to one of the batteries and charged it up. Fully charged, the engine roared to live we were off. Well, maybe it wasn't the alternator. Although, I did mention to Tarry that maybe we ought to keep the engine running when stopping for gas or a rest stop. "No worries. I 'll take care of it" he replied.

So we drove along making our way out of the National Park and everything seemed cool. Tarry said he knew of a scenic shortcut that would get us back to Windhoek about one pm and if there was time, he would conduct a little tour of his town. O.K. fine by us because our flight didn't leave until 6 p.m.

We drove north from our lodge to a road junction called Solitaire. There we would turn off onto a backroad, C-24, to go over a range of mountains that would take us to Rehoboth, a major town near Windhoek.

But wait, before we turned off, we had to gas up at an oasis of sorts outside of Solitaire known as the Bakery. Can you imagine a gourmet bakery in the middle of nowhere, renowned for its apple pie/strudel? According to Tarry, the place was built by a Scotsman, Moose McGregor. When we arrived, we could see that this oasis was indeed a lively spot with a parking lot jammed with vehicles and a few scenic wreaked vehicles out front. The layout included a general store, a bakery, a small lodge and the only gas station for miles around with the warning of gas up here or else!

**Solitaire Bakery**

While Tarry was gassing up and at the same time keeping the engine running, Yvonne and Vanessa hit the ladies' room and I wandered around the dusty, sunbaked grounds. It did have some shade trees with picnic tables but no pool. This oasis reminded me of similar ones in the outback of Australia. They are all kind of cozy, comforting places, a refuge from the wilds just a few meters away.

Finally, I made my way over to the bakery and bought a large chunk of what appeared to be a piece of apple strudel and a coffee to go. I sat down with the others at a picnic table and munched away. Of course, the apple-whatever was delicious.

Soon we were on the road again, turning onto C-24 which shortly turned into a tortuous road over hill and dale on inclines that would challenge a mountain goat. Tarry had to put the vehicle in the lowest of low gear as we ground our way to the top. Believe or not, Tarry said ranchers lived among these isolated hills and valleys in order to graze their cattle on its comparatively green slopes.

Upon reaching the highest point of this hilly terrain, Tarry pulled into a viewing spot and inadvertently shut off the engine. Oh shit, here we were in the middle of nowhere with the engine off, I thought. I was sure it would never start it up again.

Reading my mind, Tarry looked at me and said "no worries," and proceeded to start the engine up with no trouble. Relief. Then he added, "You know, I don't think it is a battery issue at all. I think it's a problem with the alternator."

I'm thinking, "No shit, Tarry, that's even worse. If the alternator goes, we are really fucked out here."

"Worst case scenario," he continued cheerfully, "We would have to call for another safari van to come out here. We are only about two hours from Windhoek. But I am going to keep the engine running just to be safe."

"O.K," I say somewhat relieved. Meanwhile, Vanessa and Yvonne were out on the viewpoint admiring the vista and the few scattered buildings of the ranches below.

**Hill Country**

An hour later, we finally left C-24 and hit the main route to Windhoek from Rehoboth. From here on it was smooth sailing on a major highway and we soon reached the outskirts of Windhoek. Since it was early afternoon, Tarry offered us a short tour of his town, a very modern, clean, tidy looking town as only the Germans can build. He drove to the city center pointing out various government buildings and the Christuskirche, the unofficial symbol of the city, a massive German Lutheran Church.

**Windhoek**

After that Tarry drove by the Independence Memorial Museum with a big statue out front of the first president of Namibia, Sam Nujoma. Behind him was the Genocide Memorial which commemorated the atrocities that the German troops carried out against the Namibians in the early 20th century. (Maybe that was practice for a later war.)

At this point, I asked Tarry, in view of the overwhelming African majority in Namibia, did the whites still have any power in the country? As you can see, I am far from being a diplomat.

He explained at length that economically, the whites still had the majority of power. However, when it came to politics, the Namibians ruled even though there were a few white representatives in the parliament. In spite of that everyone seemed to get along unlike South Africa. The whites were pretty good at spreading the wealth around and hiring qualified Namibians. In any case, there wasn't the militancy here among Namibian blacks that you had in South Africa. Compared to most

African countries, the per capita income here was much higher with the exception of Botswana. It was about three thousand dollars per person.

Continuing he said, "You have seen for yourself, how prosperous many of the smaller towns here are. In short, what with booming tourism, it's a good time for Namibia."

I thought Tarry should work for the Namibia chamber of commerce. But hey, he was a patriotic guy.

Finishing off our little driving tour, Terry pointed down a residential street saying that's where his parents lived and then turning a corner we went by his old private school. He told us the only reason he was able to go there was that he didn't have to pay tuition since his mother taught there. "That's about ten thousand a year U.S." He then pointed to an office on a little square in this residential area, saying that was the main office for Ultimate Safaris, and adding, "All the trucks and other stuff are in a maintenance yard outside of town."

Nonetheless, overall, if you were white, it seemed to me that living in Namibia was a cozy, tight-knit affair and overall, a pretty good deal.

Our little tour done, Tarry drove us out to the airport. We got there around 3 p.m. and unloaded. Tarry took a couple of bags and I took mine and we trooped on into the terminal. There we discovered that the South African check-in desk was closed and wouldn't open until four so we loaded our stuff up on a cart and retired to a restaurant area for a bite of lunch, this time on the Browns. Tarry joined us for a bit and then excused himself, saying he had to get back to the office, he had some catch-up work to do.

We shook hands with Tarry and again expressed our gratitude for his stellar role as a driver-guide throughout Namibia, truly sorry to see him go. It was almost like having a member of a family leaving us.

\*\*\*

We finally checked into our flight to Cape Town around 4 p.m. and at 5:30 we began to board the plane, a little piss-ant jet, cramped and crowded to the gills. Welcome to South Africa's subsidiary airline, Airlink. With only two seats per row, this was a real commuter plane. They did manage to serve a dinner of sorts, some pasta crap with chunks of chicken. However, beer and wine were free. It was a two-hour flight to Cape Town but it felt longer because there were no entertainment units in the seatbacks.

I didn't care because I had brought my electronic Nook along and was now reading *How to Steal a Country: State Capture and Hopes for Future of South Africa* which chronicled South Africa's corrupt politics since the end of apartheid. The author was a former British Ambassador, Robin Renwick who had been on hand at the ending of apartheid.

What he described wasn't a pretty sight. It was best summarized by Archbishop Desmond Tutu who said when it came to the ruling ANC party, rather than derail the "gravy train" of the white power structure in South Africa, the top ANC members merely climbed on board and continued the looting of various state-run industries such as utilities and power plants. They called this phenomenon, "State Capture."

However, according to Renwick, now there may be hope since they got rid of the longtime president, Jacob Zuma, universally acknowledged to be the most corrupt of them all. Elected to this post was now a longtime politician known as being relatively clean, Cyril Ramaphosa. Renwick said that he would see but that early indications were that Ramaphosa was trying to clean out the corruption by a series of controversial moves which we will go into later.

***

By and by, we landed at the Cape Town International Airport. However, when I looked out my window I saw that we had taxied up to an area on the tarmac that was far from the terminal building. What gives?

Tired and grumpy, we were in no mood to trek across this tarmac, especially since it was raining hard. But worry not, exclaimed one of the attendants, there was a bus that would take us to the terminal at the customs entrance. No shit. Still, how bush that there was no rampway to extend out to the plane from the terminal.

We unloaded from the plane and climbed aboard a crowded bus and were shuttled to the customs entrance. At first, I wondered why customs? Then I realized that we were in a different country from Namibia. This was an example of each little bush league country in Africa jealously guarding its sovereignty. I wondered why Namibia, Botswana and South Africa hadn't formed a European type union allowing one to go from one border to another unhindered.

Luckily, customs was perfunctory and quick and we were out in no time to the main part of the terminal. And there with a sign inscribed with the familiar "3 Browns" was a greeter from Lillo Travel holding it up. Hey, this really works, going first class, I had to admit. The greeter, Leonard, led us out, after loading our stuff onto a cart to his van in the parking lot. There we loaded up and relaxed. It was now about 8:30 p.m.

The drive into Cape Town was not too bad even in the rain. I noticed that the infrastructure of roads and expressways was excellent, better than most American cities, especially Chicago where we had spent 35 years of our adult life working.

The city itself was lit up like Christmas sparkling in the dark until it met the bay, Table Bay. Soon we arrived at our destination on the waterfront. We were staying at the Victoria & Alfred hotel right on the water. We had picked it because it was in the middle of the waterfront action of Cape Town and also because it was safe with lots of security around. More about that later.

**Victoria & Alfred Hotel**

The hotel struck us a big barn of a place. It wasn't the most expensive hotel on the waterfront but good enough. Three stars, I suppose. We entered the main entrance through a long corridor lined with shops. Eventually, we arrived at the reception desk. They had been expecting us and everything was in order. The young lady at the desk was crisp and efficient and we soon had our room keys, our luggage already taken and placed in our rooms.

Meanwhile, I noticed that it was awfully noisy in the reception area. A lot of the laughing and joking was going on a bar just steps from the reception desk. I glanced over and saw a sunken restaurant lounge, very expansive, that looked out on a dock and waterfront. Several boats were lined up at the dock as well. They weren't kidding when they said "waterfront hotel." I would check that out later.

Now to our rooms which were on the first floor, one floor up from the reception area. And yes all that noise in the bar did indeed filter up to our floor. Hmmm. I didn't know if this would work out for us. In some ways, a first-floor room was convenient because we didn't have to use the elevators which I had already notice were extremely slow. Instead, there was a wide staircase right next to them that we could use. But what about the noise?

When Yvonne and I entered the room, I shut the door and voila, the noise vanished. It was like we were in our own little silent cocoon. Older hotels like this had thick walls and thick soundproof doors. Plus the room looked out on a lively street scene, the noise of which still did not penetrate. Vanessa phoned us telling us that her room was quiet too and that she was going to bed. Yvonne said she was doing the same. It was almost ten but I was still hungry so I went down to the mayhem of the bar and ordered a beer and started helping myself to various free hors-d'oeuvres.

Sitting on a nearby couch, I checked out the scene. There were many heavyset to fat, boisterous Afrikaners around, drinking and partying. I figured it must be some group from the boondocks of South Africa, because, they didn't look too sophisticated. Certainly not from Cape Town, I thought. Oh, well what you expect at a tourist hotel in the center of a tourist hotspot, the waterfront. This is what you told Karen that you wanted in Cape Town. It looked like we got it. Quite a contrast to the serenity of the bush that we had been experiencing for the past two weeks or so.

I soon finished my beer and went back to my room, calling it a day. Tomorrow a tour of the city itself.

Africa: Around the Edges

# 13. CAPE TOWN

**Wed. May 9**

The next morning, we dined at a rather sumptuous breakfast buffet with many items cooked to order—eggs, sausage, pancakes, etc. We were sitting at a table with a view of the harbor filled with yachts and various sailing vessels. We almost didn't want to leave. Alas, duty called and we adjourned to get ready for a city tour.

The Lillo tour guide showed up in reception at 9 a.m. She was a bright, little, brown skin woman in a Lillo polo shirt. I figured her as being East Indian. Her name was Avril. I complimented her on her name. "You know that's French for April don't you."

"Of course I do. My mother was in love with French names and anything French."

**Avril**

Avril led out us out to her van parked right outside the hotel and what a nice van it was. A plush Mercedes van with three rows of leather seats.

Before we left, Avril explained the itinerary for the day. "We will be going on a half-day tour of the city and if we have time some of the nearby suburbs on the oceanfront. Before we start is there anything special you would like to see?"

"No, not really," I replied. I had read about the highlights of the city but left the choices up to her.

"O.K.," she continued, "first we will head downtown to give you an idea of how modern and how bustling Cape Town is."

And with that, she drove off down the waterfront road and before long into the city center, expertly navigating the traffic. (Later we would learn Avril had once driven a taxi in Cape Town and knew all the byways and shortcuts and how to avoid bottlenecks.)

As we rolled through the heart of downtown, we noted the many new buildings, not exactly skyscrapers but tall enough. Everything looked clean and well swept. We also noticed virtual armies of African street sweepers and trash- picker-uppers clad in yellow vests. Also, here and there, official parking hosts who would direct you to a parking spot. Avril said this was all an attempt to give everyone a job in South Africa, no matter how menial. And that these Africans were proud of what they did. I thought to myself that was something that big U.S. cities like Chicago should do.

At one point near the civic buildings, we pulled into a parking lot to take a look at a magnificent old fort, the Castle of Good Hope. This bastion fort was built by the Dutch East Indies Company in the mid-17th century. You see, at that time Cape Town was merely a stopover and supply point for the Dutch traders as they made their way to the Dutch East Indies, their main source of spices worth a fortune in Europe.

*Africa: Around the Edges*

**Castle of Good Hope**

We viewed the fort from the parking area taking in its dramatic ramparts made even more dramatic by its setting with Cape Town's iconic Table Mountain in the background. After a few minutes here, we moved on further into downtown until we came to a nightclub and café area along Long Street. I had read about Long Street as a colorful area especially at night but that it also had a crime problem. Pickpockets were everywhere focusing on tourists. However, in the daylight, everything was serene and welcoming.

At this point, Avril asked us if we would like to see a special museum documenting the razing of an area known as District 6, an area that was home to Cape Town's coloreds. She was rather hesitant in asking this like maybe we weren't interested in race relations in Cape Town. She then followed up by saying her family once lived in District 6. Still thinking she was East Indian, I offered, "So East Indians lived here too?"

"Oh, a few but mostly they were a mixed-race between black and maybe Indian, maybe Asian and maybe white. Take me, I am of mixed race. My mother was black and my father was white."

"No kidding I would have thought for sure you were an East Indian."

"Yes, most people make that mistake," she replied. "I am proudly a mixed-race white and black woman which once relegated me to colored status before apartheid ended in 1994."

"Well, times must be better now," I said.

"Oh yes, we have many more opportunities but still not as many as the whites. Take my only sister, she is technically mixed-race too but she looks as white as your wife. So she was classified as white while growing up and had a lot more opportunities for a better education than I did," Avil stated matter of factly.

"Really," I said glancing at Yvonne who was mixed race herself based on the racial mixing of the Surinamese during the Dutch colonial period there. "Yes, we do want to see this museum."

**District Six Museum**

Whereupon, Avril skillfully swooped into a tight parking spot just steps from the museum housed on the ground floor of what appeared to be a former bank building. We trooped on in and got an education on a darker period of Cape Town history.

Essentially, the museum documented the forced removal of 60-thousand inhabitants of various races from this area, known as District 6. This occurred at the peak of the apartheid period in the 1970s.

**Interior Museum**

As we gazed, around we saw that the floor of the museum was covered with a big map of District 6 and on the walls were handwritten notes and photographs by former inhabitants pinpointing where their particular home was located. Elsewhere there were hundreds of photographs documenting the destruction of this area with bulldozers and wrecking balls running amuck tearing buildings apart. It reminded me of the Israelis tearing into the homes of Palestinians to make way for the expansion of their own settlements.

**Apartheid Sign**

Surrounding the ground floor was a second-floor balcony on the walls of which were more photographs of individual homeowners who had been removed from District 6 along a lot of official-looking documentation from the Cape Town government justifying the destruction of District 6. The basic rationale was that the place was a slum and that it had to be replaced by much better housing which eventually it was many years later. However, most of the original residents never returned and were forced to live in townships. (One of which we would see later.)

After a half hour in this depressing museum, we met up with Avril who had been waiting in the van and she took us over to a well-known gourmet bakery a couple of blocks away from where we had a coffee and a couple of delicious sweet rolls. Yvonne exclaimed, "My, is this just like the Germans or the Dutch bake, not like the oversweet crap produced by American bakeries."

Following our coffee break, Avril drove up a nearby hill behind the business section into a colorful residential area. The townhouses were painted in an array of pastel colors like you might find in some towns in the Caribbean. Many of the streets were still paved in cobblestone. The whole area dated back to the 18th century. Avril said that this was the Muslim section of town known as the Bo-Kaap or the Malaya Quarter.

Muslims? I never realized that South Africa had Muslims. But it made sense. Many Muslims came from Southeast Asia and East India. Most came forcibly as slaves or indentured labor. Later some came voluntarily. All were Muslim and clung to their faith as attested to by the several ornate mosques that we passed. Vanessa was particularly entranced by the area and wanted to come back to photograph it some more.

**Malay Quarter**

Following our drive through the Malay quarter, Avril said we had only a short time left for our half-day tour. It was now 11 a.m. It was supposed to end at noon but she said since she didn't have a tour date the rest of the day, she would push it to one, giving us time to check out Table Mountain and one of the more the upscale residential sections on the oceanfront but still within Cape Town.

Vanessa was especially anxious to scout out Table Mountain since she wanted to hike up it in a couple of days. Yvonne and I wanted to see it too. Avril cautioned that we wouldn't have time to take the cable car up but we could drive up to its terminal base and get a good idea of what it offered. So we set off, up yet another hill. A lot of hills on the outskirts of Cape Town. It reminded me of San Francisco plus you could get great views of Town Bay which Cape Town fronted.

We followed Tafelberg Road up to the base of Table Mountain where the terminal building for the cable cars was located. This was not a sterile terminal area. It was a terminal area replete with many shops and restaurants and elevated viewing points. You could get a good view even from here of Cape Town below on this sparkling clear day.

Looking up, Table Mountain was clear which was not always the case according to Avril. It was often covered in clouds or fog. A pity we were not going to the top today.

**Table Mountain**

Referring to a brochure later, I learned that Table Mountain was a flat top sandstone mountain, a sandstone that was extremely resistant to erosion. Back some 510 million years it arose from the seabed forming along with other rises, a range of low-level mountains. Table Mountain was about a kilometer high and three kilometers from end to end. This relatively squat looking mountain, while scenic, was also deadly. It is said more hikers die scaling or descending this mountain than on Mt. Everest. Of course, Yvonne and I had no plans to scale the mountain. A gondola ride was good enough for us. Vanessa was another story. She planned to climb up its heights day after tomorrow. O.K. we would see.

We spent a few moments wandering around taking in the scenery before Avril signaled it was time to move on. From this base area, we drove through the park-like setting of upper Signal Hill and down towards the ocean, a crystal blue ocean today with a milky white surf. Soon were traveling along Victoria Drive which later morphed into Beach Road. This was a waterfront highway through the most exclusive and expensive real estate of the Cape Town area.

**Beach Drive**

As we passed through Bantry Bay and Clifton and other seafront communities, we saw elegant mansions perched on hillsides overlooking the ocean. Avril mentioned that this was where the rich and famous of Cape Town lived. She pointed out the high stone walls visible from the street that fronted these abodes. The walls were often topped by barbed wire and in some cases, broken glass and of course remote cameras were everywhere. Security was still a big deal in Cape Town. And indeed, based on my reading and recent news reports, I knew that there was a crime wave going on here, mostly the theft of private property but also an occasional murder of a white person to say nothing of the rampant and unsolved murders of scores of black Africans.

Beach Road eventually morphed into a city expressway that took us back to the waterfront. Again I was impressed with the highway infrastructure. Nothing tacky here. All fresh and maintained. Indeed, Avril had said that investments were pouring into Cape Town much of it from foreign sources. Also, tourism was booming.

Avril let us off at the hotel and informed us that she would be our tour guide in two days for an all-day tour of the South African wine country plus some other interesting sights that she had in mind. Was that all right with us? We said of course. We thought she was a great tour guide, this little woman with an encyclopedic knowledge of Cape Town including the history of District 6. We told her that we looked forward to seeing her in two days.

Now, what were we going to do for two days without Lillo Tours? Technically we would be on our own for the first time in Africa. Well, we had plans. I put on my independent traveler's hat and sketched it out. Tomorrow, we would take a ferry to Robben Island to see the prison that housed Nelson Mandela for 18 of his 23-years in prison. The next day, we would try to conquer the heights of Table Mountain.

What we did do the rest of this day was chill in our rooms until four or so and then we went back out to see what we could see of the waterfront attractions.

Right outside our door was an African band drumming away with ear-splitting noise. A half-block from the hotel was a giant Ferris wheel which promised fantastic views of the harbor and the city but the lines were long so we gave it a pass.

Then we walked over to an indoor mall that featured everything you might find in a mall in the U.S.—clothing shops, shoe shops, a bookstore, chain restaurants, wireless shops, etc.

After that, we hiked back along an alleyway lined with bars. One billed itself as a daycare spot for husbands, i.e. hubby could stay here and drink, play video games and listen to music while his wife shopped. Yvonne and I found that amusing.

Then heading back towards the hotel, we came upon a big square frame that framed the waterfront and Table Mountain in the background. It was a favorite photo spot. Tourists could sit on the square and have their pictures snapped.

Across the plaza, was a barn-like building that was said to house some of the best African artifacts in the city, the African Trading Post. Yvonne wanted to go in and check it out immediately but I told her later. I first wanted to scout out the ferry terminal nearby that we had to check into tomorrow for our ferry ride to Robben Island across Table Bay. I talked to an information clerk still stationed at her post inside the terminal building and she filled us in. "You should get here early because later the lines will be long. For a 9 a.m. departure, get here by 8 a.m."

"Shit," I thought. "This sounds like a project." I had had enough of this getting up early and rushing off during our safari days. But what could we do? We had to be there early.

After the ferry terminal, we spotted a fish and chips take-out joint and not wanting to spend much time and money dining, we opted for this cheap alternative but we didn't take it out. We just sat in the little, cramped eating area. Following our fish and chips, we started back to the hotel but Yvonne insisted that she wanted to explore the African Trading Post right then, so Vanessa went ahead to the hotel and I went with Yvonne into the barn.

**African Trading Post**

Inside Yvonne discovered three floors of stuff, much of it tourist junk but also some authentic African masks and other authentic African paraphernalia. I soon got bored perusing the offerings and went back downstairs to wait in an easy chair they had thoughtfully provided for bored husbands. While sitting there I noticed a rack of baseball caps. One cap had the symbol of South Africa on it along with an embroidered image of a lion. A little ostentatious I thought but I liked it and it was well made so I bought it.

**African Artifacts**

By and by, Yvonne came down the stairs, exclaiming about the finds she had made.

"Allan, I have to come back here and seriously shop for something authentic. They have much to choose from. As you know, you still owe me another birthday present."

"Yes, I know but enough already. Let's go back to the hotel and go to bed."

So that's what we did. Sleepy-bye and end of day one in Cape Town. Tomorrow Robben Island.

# 14. ROBBEN ISLAND

**Thur. May 10**

The next morning after being well breakfasted again, we were out early trekking over to the ferry terminal for our voyage to Robben Island. As the info lady had predicted there was already a long line for the 9 a.m. Ferry, a line that quickly got a lot longer after we arrived with mostly tourists like us. Many were bundled up as if they were going to the Antarctic. We had on down vests and light down jackets to ward off the cold too.

Meanwhile, we stood in line waiting patiently or almost patiently. I broke away and wandered around the terminal. It was a modern affair with a lot of plate glass windows and rampways. The walls had many photos of the old terminal and the ferries of yore. Eventually, I rejoined the line and held our place while Vanessa and Yvonne explored around. I had brought my Nook along and soon was engrossed in the last chapters of *Cry of the Kalahari*. Indeed, our days on safari were fast fading in our minds in view of all this new urban stimuli of Cape Town. Our safaris were acquiring an almost a surreal aspect and I was not quite sure if it had actually happened.

Vanessa and Yvonne returned and lo, a couple of officious looking clerks placed themselves at the head of the line right at the turnstile and started to let people in if they had tickets. If not they had to go buy them at the ticket counter and then get in at the back of the line. This procedure seemed to me a rather haphazard affair but soon we handed our tickets over and went through the turnstile and walked on out the dock where the ferry was waiting. It was a rather small ferry; certainly not one that carried cars and it had seen better days. But I guessed it would get us to the Robben Island which was about eight miles offshore. We all went up to the upper enclosed deck where it was cozy warm and sat down.

There was a small snack shop here and I ordered a round of coffees. We sat down and sipped coffee as the ferry pulled out from the dock into the choppy waters of Table Bay.

By and by, we were a good distance from the waterfront and could look back at the city and at Table Mountain looming behind. With the sun glancing through the clouds, brightening up the whole scene, you could see what a picturesque tableau Cape Town presented from the sea. I could imagine those early Dutch sailors being impressed with the scene, of course minus the town, and eager to get on dry land after weeks of sailing in the treacherous Atlantic currents along the coast of West Africa.

**Cape Town Waterfront**

Although Robben Island was only eight miles offshore, it took our slow-moving ferry almost an hour to traverse the distance. I guess the hamsters in the engine room were tired this morning. I noted with envy another tour boat, a hydrofoil, blasting past us at top speed. I assumed it too was heading to Robben Island. How come we didn't know about that? It probably cost a lot.

Nevertheless, we did finally make it to Robben Island which from a distance appeared to be a low lying flat island barely visible above the sea. I wondered if it had ever been hit by a hurricane.

**Robben Island**

Once docked, everyone trooped off the ferry and climbed into waiting buses that would take us to the prison grounds. Well, almost every bus. The bus we climbed into had no driver. In fact, a bunch of drivers was milling around talking animatedly. It turned out that they were substitute drivers because the regular bus drivers had gone on strike. Even so, there were not enough substitute drivers to go around.

Many buses just sat here but with no available driver. A supervisor showed up after a while and told us that we should be patient and that we would have a driver by and by. I was ready to walk. I mean how far could it be? I could see the prison gate about a quarter-mile away. Easy stroll, I thought. Just about the time that I convinced Yvonne and Vanessa to take the short hike, a driver did show up and climbed into the bus driver's seat.

Soon we were off. The bus traversed the short distance and parked in a lot right outside the prison walls. We disembarked and stood at the main entrance to the actual prison which was surrounded by intimidating stone walls and guard towers perched at strategic spots adjacent to the walls. This was a prison in the most dreadful sense of the word.

**Robben Gate**

While we waited for our tour guide to show up, I reviewed a flyer that I had picked up at the info desk at the ferry terminal that gave a little history of Robben Island. It was used as a prison as soon the Dutch arrived in the 17th century. They sent mainly political prisoners from the Dutch East Indies. When the British took over the Cape in the early 1800s, they too used the island as a prison for those who resisted their rule, mainly various local tribal chiefs.

Later in the 1850s and on, Robben Island became a leper colony until the Second World War when the island was used as a military base. Following the institution of apartheid in 1948, it once again became a prison for political prisoners and remained that way until the end of apartheid in 1994. It was interesting to note that occasionally someone did escape from the prison and managed to survive the frigid waters, the sharks and the rocks surrounding the island. The earliest known escapee to survive was a convict called Jan Rykman in 1690.

Finally, a big jolly-looking African came out and introduced himself as John. During his introductory spiel in a hard to follow accent, John told us that he had been a prisoner himself for several years for so-called political crimes. "As a result, I know this place quite well," he joked.

**Guide John**

John then led us into the prison proper. We marched down a long, dark hallway and into a courtyard surrounded by those high intimidating walls. There he gave a brief history of the prison and invited us to look around the courtyard. John said it had been a place of assembly and inspection for contraband, but also a place for exercise and recreation for the prisoners. There was even a little garden at the far end that the prisoners tended, hoping for fresh vegetables.

**Courtyard**

At one point, Yvonne asked John how a prisoner such as Mandela, as well educated as he was, kept intellectually alive all the time he was in the prison. John said that surprisingly, Mandela did have access to reading material some of which was smuggled in from the outside such as a copy of Shakespeare's complete works.

"This place wasn't a locked-down dungeon from the middle ages," he claimed. "In fact, many of the young white guards who worked here came to regard Mandala, as kind of a saint during his 18 years here. He was considered a model prisoner, causing no trouble. About the harshest thing the prisoners had to do was work in a rock quarry outside the prison and even that was popular as I will explain later."

After the courtyard, John led us through the cellblock where the prisoners actually lived. At first glance, these tiny cells were shocking, only about eight by seven feet in dimension. All they had inside were one thin fiber mat over the concrete floor upon which to sleep, a thin blanket, a small table with eating utensils and a bucket for a toilet. That was it. No chairs, no running water. John pointed out Mandela's former cell and it was identical to all the others. I thought to myself, no wonder the prisoners liked to hang out in the courtyard or even the quarry.

**Mandela's Cell**

Following this short tour through the prison, we were loaded back onto the buses to get a look at the rest of the island. Our first stop was the quarry that John had mentioned. It was a rather small quarry but you could still see the remnants of the stones that the prisoners had broken apart by a sledgehammer. Surprisingly, John said this was a popular place for the prisoners. They liked being outdoors for hours at a time and they liked the conditioning they underwent while breaking up the rocks, but most importantly, they liked the light supervision by only a guard or two and they had plenty of time to confer with each other.

**The Quarry**

John claimed that Mandela conducted the equivalent of social justice seminars with the other prisoners while cracking open rocks. Amazingly, some of his most interested bystanders were the white guards themselves who knew first-hand about the injustices of the apartheid system.

Now I paused and wondered if John was giving us the straight scoop on the prison. He sounded Pollyannaish to me making some aspects of imprisonment seem so pleasant. Like did the prisoners really enjoy splitting rocks especially since they knew the material would never be used for construction? Even John told us that. Also, were the white guards that indulgent with the political prisoners who were actually advocating the overthrow of the white apartheid government? Even Mandela in his early years advocated violence. Who knew? But I figured that if John had been more honest about prison life on Robben Island, he wouldn't be a tour guide here.

Moving on, John pointed out a small subdivision of bungalows that were once the homes of the guards and other prison officials. Now, he said many of them were used as guesthouses for tourists who wanted to stay overnight. In fact, moves were afoot to make Robben Island a tourist destination with all kinds of recreational opportunities. Indeed, we did pass some beach-like settings but to me, the surf looked far too wild for swimming or surfing.

However, Robben Island was also known as a nature lover's paradise with its unique flora and fauna with over a hundred species of birds, including cormorants and herons which bred on the island in large colonies. Once in a while, a penguin or a seal would show up and you might catch a glimpse of a Southern Right Whale just offshore.

Finally, after our short tour of the island, it was time for a coffee and bathroom break. And lo, at the far end of the island was a building on the seashore that housed a snack bar, a café and of course bathrooms. It also offered good views of the sea and back towards the city. We spent about twenty minutes here and then reloaded on the bus. Minutes later we were back at the ferry terminal where our ferry was waiting for us.

Clockwork, just like clockwork, I thought. We had barely spent more than two hours on this island. We had arrived at ten and it was now past noon. By 1 p.m. our ferry had us back at the Cape Town waterfront.

***

Essentially, we had no real plans for the rest of the day. What to do? Well, we killed the time by wandering around the waterfront pier some more, then resting and then eating dinner at a little Italian restaurant next to the hotel. They had a special on lasagna and it was quite good, especially with a cheap bottle of Chianti to wash it down.

Following dinner, I accompanied Vanessa to the hotel tour desk to "help" set up her hike up Table Mountain tomorrow. Right off the bat, the tour desk clerk asked her if she wanted a guide or not. The conversation went like this.

**Vanessa**: I'm not sure. How well marked are the trails?
**Clerk**: Not bad, it depends which one you take, an easy trail or a more challenging one.
**Vanessa**: Well, I don't want the easiest or the hardest.
**Clerk**: So what about a guide?
**Vanessa**: Do I really need one?
**Clerk**: I generally recommend one for first-time hikers even on the easy trail.
(At this point I chimed in.)

**Allan:** Yes, Vanessa, I agree with the tour specialist. You need a guide. I've read that a lot of people get lost climbing up Table Mountain, some of them even die.

**Vanessa:** Dad, I don't need your unwanted advice. Remember I hiked the Mont Blanc trail in France by myself for a week last summer. But yes, I am thinking about a guide. How much would that cost?

**Clerk:** Well, a guide for a half-day hike would be U.S. $250, well worth it, I think.

**Vanessa:** That's a lot of money.

**Clerk:** Yes, the price would be lower per person if you had another person in your party,
( the clerk said glancing at me.)

**Allan:** Don't look at me. My wife and I are taking the cable car tomorrow.

Finally, Vanessa said, "O.K." and she handed over her credit card. The clerk ran it through and as he did so he assured Vanessa that he would get a competent, well-experienced guide for her. He also instructed her that she had to be ready to go at 8 a.m. And that the hike would probably take at least three hours. Finally, she had to be fully prepared with water, sunscreen, possibly a raincoat, and good hiking shoes.

Wow, I thought. That sounded like a major trek. I was glad that Vanessa was going with a guide and I was also glad that Yvonne and I were taking the cable car instead.

Following our little tour arrangement, we retired to our rooms and that was the end to our Robben Island day in Cape Town. Tomorrow Table Mountain.

# 15. TABLE MOUNTAIN

**Fri. May 11**

After an early breakfast, Vanessa and I were at the tour desk waiting for her guide even though Table Mountain was socked in with fog and clouds. Right on the dot of 8 a.m., he showed up. At first glance, I thought, this can't be. This guy looked like he belonged in a tribal rock band. He was tall and skinny with light brown skin and had a wild dreadlock hairdo wrapped in a bun on the top of his head that was secured with a colorful tribal ribbon.

He had a big smile and introduced himself as Moke, at our service. I was surprised that he spoke in a clipped British accent. He sounded well-educated. Later we would learn that Moke had worked in hi-tech for years in Britain and here in South Africa before becoming a mountain guide. One of the first things that he did upon meeting us was to show us his mountain guiding credentials for Table Mountain.

Vanessa was visibly impressed by the dude and I sensed that he had to be competent looking like that. At first, he assumed that I was coming along but we set him straight on that matter. After a quick briefing with Vanessa assuring her that the fog on Table Mountain would soon disappear, he checked out her gear and then they were off in his little VW beetle.

I returned to the room to discuss the day's activities with Yvonne. Seeing the foggy weather at breakfast, she had changed her mind about going up Table Mountain. She told me that all she wanted to do today was shop at the African Trading Post, look at diamonds in the nearby jewelry stores and chill.

"You're not going to see much of the mountain with it being socked-in by clouds and fog," she asserted.

"Yeah," I replied, "maybe, but this is our only chance to go up to the top. And it might clear up later. Come on."

"No," she replied. "You go ahead. I want a day to myself."

I didn't argue with her. She obviously had her own agenda for the day and didn't want me around. I guess we needed space from each other. In any case, I was eager to go up Table Mountain fog, clouds or whatever. This day would probably be my only chance. I mean, how can you come to Cape Town and not go to the top of Table Mountain? Thus, I geared up with a down vest, a light jacket over it and my little Casio camera that I had not used yet on this trip.

Outside the hotel, I got into a cab that was sitting there and twenty minutes later I was at the base terminal for the Table Mountain cable cars. Before I entered the terminal, I looked around at the view and had to agree with Yvonne that it was pretty shitty, all fogged in. Oh, well, we will see what we can see.

I bought my ticket, hiked up some stairs to the loading area and waited for the next cable car to arrive. From what I could tell, there were two cable cars operating, one going up while the other was coming down.

As I waited in the designated waiting area with a few other European tourists, we were joined by a mob of young Koreans with cameras and decked out in logo splattered outerwear. They were a most obnoxious bunch, pushing their way around trying to get to the front of the loading area or running around snapping pictures or taking video all the time, no matter who got in the way.

The European tourists stood around stunned, most giving way to this crew, but I, who had encountered this before in Australia with a pushy Chinese group, stood my ground right up in front of the loading area.

As noted before, I am a big guy, 6-2, 230 pounds, hard to move. However, these Koreans were small and slight but very agile as they snapped away. They simply ignored me and infiltrated into tiny open spaces like little rats.

Moments later our cable car arrived, opened its doors and crush, the Koreans pushed on in working around the European tourists, except for me. I got in fast and secured a spot at the window that would give me a view of the valley below as we went up.

A little Korean girl with a camera tried to wiggle in between me and the window, but I firmly but gently pushed her aside. She gave me a blank look and then tried to wiggle in elsewhere. As we took off up the mountain, I continued to hold my ground and started snapping pictures myself, but I still had to watch it because one kid, a large kid for a Korean, tried to push in and almost made it because I was fooling with my camera. I stopped him short with an elbow to the chest and he backed off.

What gives with these Koreans? They act as if you aren't there. If I had clobbered one or two of them, I am sure they would have ganged up on me or start accusing me of being a racist.

Remind me never to go to the Asian mainland, especially China or Korea. A couple of years ago, we did go to Japan but we found the Japanese to be polite and considerate and not pushy at all except when getting on their trains at rush hour. Despite the Koreans, I did manage to take some photographs but the view was limited due to the fog/clouds.

**Foggy Day**

The ride on the cable car was fairly short about fifteen minutes. Once at the upper terminal, it was fogged in and cold. You could barely see a few yards ahead of you, but I did notice that it came and went. Very weird. The locals say Table Mountain makes its own weather regardless of what the weather is elsewhere. No shit, I thought. I zipped up my jacket and sallied forth.

Meanwhile, the Koreans had scrambled off and ran up the walkways to the various viewpoints surrounding the terminal and continued snapping away. Let them have it. I headed for the shelter of the restaurant and concession complex for a hot chocolate before I explored around.

As I did so, who should I run into but Vanessa and Moke. They had just finished their hike. It had only taken them two and a half hours. That's quick for a climb up Table Mountain.

"So how did it go?"

"Not bad, a lot of scrambling, in fact mostly scrambling," Vanessa replied. "But Moke is a great guide and he showed me the way. Nobody was on the trail so we went fast."

Moke chimed in, "Vanessa is a great scrambler. No problems at all. She could easily do harder trails."

We retired to the café and had a round of hot chocolate while Moke filled us in on his life. He said he had married a German girl a few years ago. Now he was pushing 45 and was a dad for the first time in his life. We chatted some more about life in Cape Town and the outdoor adventures that awaited should we choose to take advantage of them. I thanked Moke profusely for shepherding Vanessa safely up the mountain, much to Vanessa's embarrassment.

Finally, we said goodbye to Moke, explaining that Vanessa would go down with me and back to the hotel once we toured around the top. By now the clouds/fog had lifted a little and we hiked around the paved trails to different viewpoints. Except we kept running into those crazy Koreans.

The Korean that I had elbowed came running by snapping pictures of everything and everyone in sight. At first, I didn't see much that was interesting to photograph. The terrain was bleak, filled as it was with embedded rocks and scrub bushes. Even so, I took a photo of Vanessa, the conquer of Table Mountain.

**Vanessa on Top**

I suppose there was a lot of unique flora here, but it didn't register on us. Rather, we focused on little squirrely like creatures scurrying over the rocks here and there. For this, we stopped and snapped a few more photos. Vanessa claimed that somehow they were related to elephants.

**Rock Hyrax**

A nearby info plaque declared that this creature known as a Rock Hyrax was indeed the closest living relative to the modern-day elephant and sea cow. Supposedly all three are descended from a common ancestor millions of years ago based on their teeth, leg and foot bones.

You don't say. Darwin's evolution is sometimes very weird. But then it has been proven that the descendants of dinosaurs are said to be still living with us, namely the birds."

After making the rounds of the viewpoints on top of Table Mountain, Vanessa and I took the cable car down to the base terminal. Just as we were leaving, the clouds had parted and we had some spectacular views of Cape Town and the surrounding area with the sparkling cobalt sea of Table Bay off in the background. We hopped a cab and were soon back at our hotel and it was only early afternoon. We decided to have a late lunch of fish and chips with a beer and after that, both were ready to retire to our separate rooms for a rest.

Yvonne was still out so I rested for an hour until she returned with her latest purchases; this time with another fertility statue which she assured me was a remarkable find. No doubt it was since Yvonne is rather an expert in these matters as a former professional art librarian at the Chicago Public Library.

I was now restless and wanted to explore the waterfront area some more and take a few more pictures. I hooked up with Vanessa and went out to the dock in back of our hotel and took a careful look at a rather dated yacht called "Jackie O." In front of the yacht was a billboard advertising B & B lodging. Although dated, this 90-foot yacht was in beautiful condition, all refurbished, newly painted, its brass fixtures gleaming in the afternoon sun. I briefly wondered if this was the original yacht that Jackie sailed around on with Aristotle Onassis. It appeared to fit the time period of the 1960s.

**"Jackie O"**

By and by, a well-dressed gentleman in a nautical outfit came out of the main cabin and up the plank. I asked him if this was the original Onassis yacht. He said that this was not the same yacht but it was a twin yacht built about the same time. I asked if Jackie Onassis had ever sailed on it. He said no. She sailed on the other identical yacht, the "Christina O." named after Onassis's daughter.

He explained that he was the owner and had just refurbished this yacht and was now using it as a bed and breakfast. Was I interested? I said maybe and took a brochure from him. $300 bucks a night. Rather steep I thought. I thanked him, pocketed the brochure and moved on.

Further down towards the end of the waterfront, past the mall, Vanessa and I ran across an old sailing ship docked at the pier.

**Europa**

It was called Europa and it was a three-masted tall ship from the days of yore. Or so we thought. It almost looked like a museum piece but several young people were scurrying about the deck cleaning it up and adjusting the rigging like it was a real working ship.

**On Deck**

Then a hippy looking, bearded dude, climbed up the gangplank, I stopped him and asked what gives with the ship.

"Nothing. We are now getting ready to return to our base in Holland with a stopover on St. Helena."

"So where have you been?"

"Lots of places around the world. Most recently Antarctica."

"You mean you can sail around Antarctica in that ship? Is it an icebreaker or something?" I asked.

"We know how to skirt the ice."

"So what does it take to get on a cruise with this ship?"

"Not much. Just a willingness to learn how to be a sailor on a tall ship, to get along with other people, and of course payment of the fare."

"Are you expected work even if you pay your way?"

"For most yes but we do have some passengers who can take it easy. Depending on the voyage."

"I guess you have to be in good shape to do this."

As he looked me over, "Yeah, we get a few people in their 60s and 70s on board. They all do pretty well."

"How much is the fare if I may ask."

"Eight to nine thousand Euros for twenty-two days."

"So what happens when there's no wind? How do you get about?"

"There's almost always a breeze. In the case of the doldrums, we have a big diesel engine to motor us about. You should know that below deck we are fully modernized for global sailing."

"I see."

In the meantime, I was checking out the regular crew still scurrying about. Yanking on ropes and checking on sails. One guy had climbed up to the crow's nest and was poking around. I'm thinking, "Yo ho, ho and a bottle of rum."

**Up in the Mast**

There was a time when I might have been tempted to go on a cruise like this, especially thirty years ago when I was in my South Seas phase. I think I had read every major piece of literature on the South Pacific for the last hundred years along with a score of sail-around-the-world books. I was definitely ready to go then but at the same time, I had a job with limited vacation time and a family—wife Yvonne, daughter Vanessa, and the new addition in 1984, Colin. So what did we do instead? We took a three-week flying trip in 1985 to the South Pacific, namely to Tahiti, Bora, Bora, Moorea, New Zealand, and a week stay on an out-island in Fiji. We spent a few brief hours in Hawaii and then it was home to Chicago. I wrote all about it in my book *Chasing After Paradise* available on Lulu.com.

Anyway, these days, I think a short, luxury inter-island sailing cruise either in the Caribbean or in French Polynesia would be about right. A long, long cruise on the Europa would be too much for Yvonne and me. Still, watching these kids go about their sailing chores, apparently not worried about their future, not worried about college, job prospects or making any real money in the real world was inspiring.

Following our nautical explorations, Vanessa and I returned to the hotel and an hour later we went out to dinner at the Italian restaurant that we had dined at the night before. This time instead of lasagna, we had delicious individual pizzas with beer. That was it for our third day in Cape Town.

Tomorrow, the South African wine country.

# 16. WINE COUNTRY

**Sat. May 12**

Upon greeting us at 8:30, and describing the day ahead, Avril wanted to know if we would like to see a nearby township before we drove out to the wine country. We said of course since we had skipped Soweto Township outside of Jo-Berg. Aside from a lingering sense of obligation to see how many South Africans lived, we were genuinely curious. Were they really as bad as often depicted in news reports?

The first thing we did was tour the Langa Township right outside Cape Town near the airport. From the main highway, it didn't look too promising for were passing by row after row of cargo containers that had been converted into housing.

Avril explained that these containers were for the new arrivals to Cape Town, mainly non-South Africans from all over Africa who had come here for work. She stressed that the government was doing its best to improve their housing.

However, once we turned into the Langa Township proper, we were traveling on paved streets lined with modest bungalows, and small businesses.

**Langa Housing**

Now, I have seen slums far worse than what we were seeing here. Here, the streets were relatively clean with late-model cars going about. This was not a deep dark slum-like you might see on Chicago's Westside.

Overall, Langa looked like a thriving but modest community doing the best that it could. Kids and adults were walking about, greeting, joking, shopping like any small ethnic neighborhood in Chicago. Indeed, as we drove along the main street, we noted that the housing became more upscale, modern and fairly prosperous-looking with fences, lawns and gardens.

Even so, Avril pointed out that times were tough for most residents. Sixty percent of the adults here were unemployed. But that didn't mean that these people didn't work. Many worked in the informal economy, either by running a Spaza shop (a township shop run out of people's homes) or by street vending. Only a few had regular jobs mostly in construction or with Cape Town city proper as street sweepers and custodians.

**Township Store**

By and by, we pulled up in front of the Guga S'thebe Cultural center that Avril desperately wanted to show us. A guy in fancy African dress greeted us and offered us a short tour of the place. We accepted and before we knew it, we were learning about the local artisans and the cultural meaning of many old artifacts of long ago tribes.

**Guga S'thebe Cultural Center**

We also saw a group of local women engaged in some sort of a cloth weaving project. The guide explained further that the cultural center offered training in metalwork, pottery and, of course, painting and sculpting. There was also a community theater and instruction in traditional dance.

As the tour ended, our guide mentioned that many of the artworks, sculptures and paintings were for sale. Hint, hint. What else could we do? Yvonne bought a nice painting for a hundred Rand (U$10.00) and I deposited an additional hundred Rand note into a donation box.

**Avril Looking**

As we made our way out of the township along a different route, Avril pointed out block after block of government housing going up, both townhouses and apartment buildings. As if to say, see, townships are not so bad and progress is being made.

Being diplomatic, I failed to inquire about the crime rate but Avril reading my mind said, "Crime happens here of course but compared to many other townships, it is not too bad. Most importantly, there is a lot of social pressure here among the residents, to be law-abiding. They keep pretty good control of the potential troublemakers."

Soon we were driving along highway N2, one of the main routes to the wine country. Along the way, I briefly wondered if the Langa Township was merely a "show township" for tourists, sort of a Potemkin village shielding the grimmer realities of other nearby townships. Well, O.K. maybe it was but maybe it was what it was and it wasn't too bad.

***

Leaving the expressway finally, we wound our way through the wine country of South Africa, a country of rolling hills dotted with vineyards with mountains in the background. Picturesque indeed. In many ways similar to the wine country of Napa Valley and Sonoma County in northern California.

**Wine Country, S.A.**

Soon we arrived at our first wine-tasting stop, the Fairview Wine and Cheese Farm.

**Fairview Winery**

We parked, got out and admired the Cape Dutch main building and then trooped on into the tasting room. This was a cavernous room with rows of counters and stools upon which to perch as a wine steward buzzed up and down pouring minute quantities of various wines into small wine glasses along with an array of cheeses on a plate. As he did so, he went into a spiel about each of the offerings.

We started out with white and kept going up to red. But after the first few tastings, I felt like spitting it out. I had indeed drunk much better South African wine while on safari. Although Fairview had a reputation of producing fine, award-winning wines, the stuff they were serving us this morning tasted like rot-gut.

Maybe my wine tasting apparatus was off or maybe not. I was not in the mood for wine tasting at 10:30 in the morning. In any case, I gave up after the first red. Yvonne and Vanessa felt the same way and we retired early from the wine tasting much to the dismay of the wine steward.

Avril, who saw what was happening suggested we go on to another nearby winery for of all things a chocolate tasting, the Bilton Winery.

*Africa: Around the Edges*

**Bilton Winery**

Over there we first had a small glass of Chenin Blanc at the wine tasting bar which was O.K. Indeed the perfect sweet wine for a morning sip and we then moved on to the chocolate. It seemed that Bilton Winery was indeed known for its vast array of homemade chocolates. Once ensconced in the chocolate tasting room, we proceed to sample very delicious but very small pieces of chocolate, washed down with a light tea. Hmm. That was tasty.

**Bilton Chocolate**

Following the chocolate tasting, we walked around the grounds a bit and then moved on to our next wine tasting adventure but by now I had no desire to taste any more South African wine.

The third winery was the Peter Falk Winery about a kilometer away. It featured a great house in the old-fashioned Cape style which had been lovingly restored. Plus the grounds were lush and stunning.

**Peter Falk Winery**

After looking around outside for a bit, we went on in but upon seeing the crowded wine tasting room, I suggested we skip the wine tasting altogether and do something else. Again, Avril stepped in and suggested a tea tasting.

"A tea tasting?"

"Yes, this establishment is known for its wide selection of teas from around the world, indeed some of them very rare and very exotic. They will also give you delicious biscuits to munch on."

O.K. that sounded good so we entered the tea room and ordered a variety of teas for the tasting. We were then instructed to go out and sit on the patio terrace where we would be served. By and by, we were served very elegantly with the chosen teacups lined up like little soldiers on a serving board. We settled in and began the samplings of our four or five different teas, the selection of which had been suggested by Avril.

**Tea Tasting**

This tasty tea along with the crunchy biscuits (cookies really) was a satisfying morning repast that gave us a burst of energy for the next sight which had nothing to do with wine, namely the nearby prison that had housed Nelson Mandala over a year before his release.

\*\*\*

A short drive later we arrived at the Victor Verster Prison where Mandela was held for fourteen months after he was transferred from Robben Island in 1988. Looking around at the grounds from the outside, we could see that this was a low-security prison compared to Robben Island. A country club prison some would say. Mandala had a bungalow to himself and reportedly had access to a swimming pool. Of course, all of this was an effort by the South African government to ease him back into society with no social disruption. Mandela was finally released in February 1990, in a dramatic exit with him walking along with his wife Winnie Mandela out the gate. Needless to say the world press was there to record the historic event.

**Press Photo: Mandela Freedom**

Located right outside the prison was a statue of Mandela commemorating his release. Note the right hand thrust up in what to me looked like a gesture of defiance. Technically, it was a black power salute. Maybe Mandela had not become so peace-loving after all.

**The Salute**

After paying our respects to Mandela and his statue, we drove on to Stellenbosch, home to the most famous university in South Africa, the Stellenbosch University. First, we drove through the university campus on the edge of town, past the usual university buildings including the dormitories which looked amazingly like Stanford University with sub-tropical palms but with a Cape Dutch touch.

**Stellenbosch University**

Walking placidly along were students who looked like students from any well-heeled American university, mostly white with a sprinkling of blacks. Avril pointed out that the official language of instruction was still Afrikaans but that moves were afoot to make English the official language throughout South Africa. Of course, the Afrikaan establishment was outraged at that prospect but based on a video that I had seen prior to coming here, most of the students, Afrikaans or not, were O.K. with English as the official language.

**Downtown Stellenbosch**

After a drive-by tour of the campus, we headed into Stellenbosch' downtown proper. Although small, it had a charming atmosphere with many restored Dutch-style buildings from the 1700s. Of course, there were all the shops and cafes and restaurants you would expect in a college town strung along the main drag.

One of the star attractions was a Dutch Reformed Church that had been built in 1866, further testifying to the Dutch/Afrikaner presence in these parts.

**Moederkerk**

By now we were hungry. After all, tea and biscuits didn't quite do it. It was now 3 p.m. so we decided to stop and have a bite to eat. We parked and then walked up and down the main street looking for a place to eat. We settled on a fish and chips joint with outdoor seating and luckily were served rather quickly.

After our late lunch, we needed a bathroom break. The joint that we ate at had no such facilities so I scouted around for a restroom and finally found one in a Dutch Cape building that had been converted into a 17$^{th}$ century pub. The place was charming and I was tempted to stop and have a beer here but Yvonne nagged me that Avril was waiting and the time was drawing near for our return to Cape Town.

On the drive back to Cape Town, I realized that we had nothing lined up for the next day. According to our schedule, it was supposed to be a day of rest after our marathon tour of Southern Africa. But shit! I still wanted to see more, especially the southernmost point on the African continent. So did Vanessa and Yvonne. I asked Avril what would it take to use her services tomorrow. She said she had to check but that as far as she knew, she was free.

Of course, she added, that we would have to be willing to pay extra for another all-day escorted tour. She then proceeded to cell phone Lillo headquarters. It turned out she wasn't scheduled for a tour so she was free to take us about. The only catch was it would cost us 400 bucks U.S. She then added that's about what we had paid for this all-day tour already. This made sense so I said that's fine with us. The deal was set: Another 400 bucks. A drop in the bucket compared to what we had already spent. Avril would be our tour guide for our last full day in Cape Town.

# 17. CAPE HOPE

**Sun. May 14**

The next morning Avril picked us up at 8:30 for a full-day tour of the Cape peninsula which featured the Cape of Good Hope, the southernmost point of Africa looking out on the vast South Atlantic. But first Avril insisted that we stop briefly at the Kirstenbosch Botanic Gardens in Table Mountain Park for a quick tour of its botanical wonders via golf cart. Our guide was a former employee now working as a volunteer. He was quite knowledgeable about all the plants especially those with medicinal properties even one that reputedly could cure syphilis.

**Syphilis Cure?**

After an informative hour riding around the park in the golf cart, we were back in Avril's van and continued on down the peninsula to the towns of Muizenberg and St. James. These were upscale communities on the oceanfront of False Bay. Avril said many people commuted from here to Cape Town. Next along was the village of Fish Hoek with a big sweeping beach and homes up on a slope overlooking the sea. We stopped and walked around its harbor full of fishing boats. It was all very picturesque.

**Fish Hoek**

After Fish Hoek, we turned up a hill and took a winding road to the Cape of Good Hope Nature Reserve, the top of which looked like a Scottish moor. We drove for several kilometers and then out onto the point for a look.

Technically this wasn't the southernmost point on the African continent. It was the most south-western point on the African continent. And what did we find? Hordes of people and cars and tour buses jammed into a little parking lot. Sightseers were all over the place, scrambling over the rocks fronting the crashing sea. All snapping pictures of the sea, the cliffs and the rocks. Of course, we did the same after squeezing into a parking spot.

Vanessa and I hiked out to a deserted spot with a good view of this most southern sea and took photos. Later I took pictures of Vanessa and Yvonne behind a sign of Cape Good Hope with the ocean in the background.

**Browns at Cape of Good Hope**

Guess what? While the setting was picturesque, the sea looked the same as the most southern ocean points in New Zealand and Australia.

**Cape Point**

Only in Chile, did it look different because when we were there we were looking at the calm Straits of Magellan. None of that mattered. For the record, I had gazed upon the Southern Ocean from four major continental points at the bottom of the world—New Zealand, Australia, Chile and now South Africa.

We spent about an hour here hiking around and then drove on, this time back toward Simon's Town for lunch. Driving down the main street, we were confronted with a picturesque tourist town with lots of knick-knack shops full of tourist paraphernalia. We picked a restaurant at random, went in and ordered fish and chips with a beer. Inside it was a hot sweaty place, with the help running around like crazy because of the lunchtime crowd.

**Simon's Town**

After lunch, we drove south of town to Boulder Beach to look at a colony of South African Penguins. In order to do so, we had to hike out on a long wooden walkway over a boulder-strewn beach until we came upon the colony. At first, I was dubious about this venture. We had seen lots of penguins in southern Chile but Avril insisted this was a sight to behold.

Coming around a bend on the boardwalk, the beach opened up and there before us were hundreds of black and white penguins waddling around tending to their colony, their eggs, etc. It was like a National Geographic special.

Avril told us that all these penguins were descended from only a few male and female penguins that were transported here from elsewhere. The transplanted penguins found the area conducive to setting up a colony and proceeded to breed and expand over the years. So while their presence here was somewhat artificial, they had indeed adopted this beach as their home and were flourishing.

*Africa: Around the Edges*

**Penguin Beach**

**Offspring**

After the penguin viewing, we returned to the van and cut over to the west side of the peninsula and drove up the M-6 coastal road which offered more spectacular views of the Southern Sea. M-6 reminded me of Highway 1 of the California coast around Big Sur. Except here, there were many more homes hanging from cliffs and of course with all the security in the world.

**Hout Bay**

We passed through towns such as Scarborough, Kommetjie, Noordhoek and Hout Bay, the latter being the most spectacular of the bunch. Then it was on to Llandudno, Camps Bay, Clifton and Sea Point that we had seen the other day. Finally, we hit the expressway heading into town and the waterfront. And that was the end of our Cape Town touring and indeed the official end of our whole wonderful trip to Southern Africa.

But wait! There was one more thing I had to do. I had to ride the giant Ferris wheel just steps from our hotel. During dinner, I proposed that we all ride the Ferris wheel to say goodbye to Cape Town but neither Yvonne nor Vanessa were interested. They said they were tired and wanted to get ready for our departure tomorrow. So I went over on my own. Luckily, there was only a short wait to get on the Ferris wheel. I climbed on and settled down for what I expected to be fantastic views of the waterfront and Cape Town all lit up at night. I was not disappointed.

Around and around went the big wheel, albeit at a very slow pace and for some reason what was supposed to be a ten-minute ride turned out to be over fifteen minutes. I guess the operator was giving us late riders a special ride.

**Waterfront Ferris Wheel**

And what views. There it was. Cape Town all lit up in the night, sparkling like diamonds across the way. A fantasy city on the water.

**Cape Town at Night**

Indeed, this whole trip had been like a fantasy. Almost unreal with its wildlife, its people and its many landmark sights. This had been a dream from which we had to wake up. For on the morrow, we were off on a flight to Jo-Berg and then back across the Atlantic to the USA.

**FIN**

# AFTERWORD

**June 2018**

O.K. The trip is done. We have been back in Colorado for a month now and reading this over, I see I have failed to go into much about the current news in South Africa during the time we were there. There was quite a lot. Reading the local newspapers, I had noticed that a bitter power struggle was going on in the Cape Town city government. The mayor Patricia de Lille was sacked last December for alleged corruption but has been fighting ever since to regain her post. It seems the white-dominated Democratic Alliance Party could not tolerate a colored mayor doing sketchy deals, including giving a Chinese company a 300-million Rand contract for electric buses. The details of this ongoing fight make Chicago politics look like a kindergarten spat.

Then there was the attack on a mosque by three Muslims in a town north of Durban. The three stormed into the local mosque stabbing people left and right, (killing one) and then fled after setting the mosque on fire. Muslims make up about 2 percent of South Africa's population most of whom are Sunnis. Police think that the attack was the result of some internal dispute among the Muslim community and not a full-fledged terrorist attack.

Even scarier has been the recent attacks on outlying farms in South Africa resulting in the murders of entire families. The most recent police statistics show that 84 people on South African farms were murdered in 2017. Of those fifty-nine were white farmers. The ruling ANC party tends to discount those numbers but is apparently doing little to stop the trend with lax police enforcement.

A lot of this is sparked by an informal policy that encourages a confiscation of white farm property with little or no compensation to the white farmers. Doesn't that sound familiar? That's exactly what happened in Zimbabwe a decade or so ago under the rule of Mugabe. As a result, Zimbabwe is in ruins economically, despite a booming tourist trade.

To further drive home the point, a few weeks after we left Cape Town, a strawberry grower near Stellenbosch in the peaceful heart of the wine country, was murdered by a gang of robbers.

Then as mentioned before, on the flight home to the U.S. we were sitting next to Hank from Utah who had gone big game hunting in South Africa. He told me that his South African guide had himself been attacked on his farm by some cutthroats over a year ago. This guide had been shot six times but survived. Hank showed us a gruesome picture of the guide's fresh wounds taken right after the attack. Chilling.

Despite its horrendous crime and murder rate, is there hope for South Africa? Some say yes since a new South African president took over, namely Cyril Ramaphosa. His stated mission was to rid South Africa of the institutional corruption condoned by the African National Congress under the leadership of Jacob Zuma. The locals refer to this corruption as "State Capture." Note that Ramaphosa has been around for years in local and national ANC governance himself but had the reputation as being above corruption. We will see. However, Ramaphosa apparently still believes in the takeover of South African land from whites, albeit legally but still without compensation. As he and many other South African blacks see it the white Afrikaners stole it all from the local tribes years ago back in the 18$^{th}$ and 19$^{th}$ centuries much like the Americans stole Indian lands in America in the 19$^{th}$ century.

Looking back all of this made me wonder if our whole tranquil trip had been a Potemkin Village tour masking the brutal and deadly realities of not only South Africa but also of Zimbabwe and yes, even prosperous-looking Namibia.

We will see. In the meantime, we will continue to nip around the edges of this African continent. It's Egypt for us in the spring of 2019.

# PART TWO

## EGYPT

# A MOMENT

Alone. All alone in one of the most isolated back chambers of the Edfu temple. This one had reliefs galore engraved on its walls. As I studied the various depictions of the different gods and goddesses, I suddenly had an eerie feeling of being tele-transported back to those ancient times.

**Edfu Relief**

I stood there for several minutes stupefied, yet soaking up the images rendering them almost life-like in my mind. Such moments were many as we made our way through the temples and monuments of Upper and Lower Egypt. All of this despite constant threats of terrorist attacks on both tourists and locals alike

"Hey, you only live once," so goes the refrain. But of course, we lived to tell the tale. And here is how it went.

# 1. FLIGHT

**Thur. Feb 28, 2019**

The Lufthansa flight from Denver took off right on time, 4:20 p.m. The only hitch was the Airbus A330-300 was crammed to the gills. We supposedly had extra legroom seats but they were not real exit row seats and thus not as much legroom. I complained that I had paid extra for exit row seats but the snotty flight attendant said there were no exit row seats available and that these seats that we were assigned had the same amount of legroom. I begged to differ. But she huffily said I could complain if I wanted but there were no exit row seats available. A further annoyance was black screening curtain hanging down right in front of us marking off the section between economy plus and regular economy. It was like flying in a shroud. The only good thing was no third seat in our row so we didn't have to contend with another seatmate.

As long as I was in the complaining mode, I noted that the inflight food was terrible and obviously cooked to American taste or rather to no taste. I was expecting at least a little bit of German cuisine.

I remembered that our Delta flight to Johannesburg via Atlanta last year was far superior. I think Lufthansa cut corners servicing Denver. The only saving grace was that this flight was nonstop to Munich, thus eliminating a layover at another U.S. airport.

Despite this general annoyance, we did manage to sleep a little but mainly we read and watched movies on the long flight to Munich.

Of course, this brings up the question of as to why we were we going to Egypt at all during these days of terrorist attacks on both tourists and Coptics. Really, it was a roll of the dice. We figured that the odds of anything happening to us were minuscule, mainly because we were assured by our tour company, Odyssey Tours, that we would have an armed security guard traveling with us at all times and that there would military security at all the major tourist sites.

"Just stick with the group and you will be fine," was the mantra. However, I should say that Odyssey did offer a full refund after the latest terrorist attack on a Coptic church two weeks before we were to leave. As it turned out only three people canceled out of a group of twenty-five.

The real reason we were going to Egypt was basically because it was there, like some sort of tourist Mount Everest to conquer. Also based on previous reading and videos about Egypt, I realized that no one could really understand the ancient civilizations of the Middle East, Greece and Rome without understanding the role Egypt played. Also the monuments such as the pyramids and temples were said to be spectacular and provided great photo ops. Add to that the fact that we had done a three-week safari in Southern Africa the year before in addition to spending a week in Cape Town. So we thought a trip to Egypt would complete the African circle, north and south, still realizing that we would only be scratching the surface of this amazing continent.

***

We landed in Munich the next morning at 9:30 a.m. right on schedule, thanks to German efficiency. We were eager to get off this crate but we now faced a six-hour layover before continuing to Cairo. Initially, I was looking forward to the layover. That time span would give us a chance to alleviate our jet lag and time to explore this city-like airport and maybe catch a high-speed train into town.

As it turned out we did nothing but mope around the International Terminal so we that would not have to go through security again. We ate, drank good German beer, read, and roamed around until we finally fell asleep in a row of reclining seats at a dark end of a deserted gate area.

During our layover, I did change some US dollars into Egyptian pounds (LE) at a ruinous rate. I had to do this because back home nobody, not even Travelex, had Egyptian pounds available in the U.S.

Around 6 p.m. we boarded our flight to Cairo. Take off was close to 7 p.m. It was a four-hour flight on a smaller plane that was also filled. We did have real exit seats this time so it wasn't too bad even if it was three across. The window seat was taken by a German businessman/engineer. He introduced himself as Oliver and said he worked for a company that built kilns for processing sugar beets, something the Egyptians grew a lot of. He was an interesting fellow, somewhere in his thirties who traveled frequently to Egypt. He spoke perfect English. He clued us in on what Cairo was like: "Really a mess. Watch out crossing streets. Pedestrians there have no rights. Don't go out alone at night and stay away from street demonstrations."

He said the Egyptians who worked at his beet processing plant tried to get it right but needed constant supervision from his company. Hence, his chore was to show up frequently and babysit. I told him I didn't envy him.

He said that while such a chore was tedious, it was a good job and paid well. Hearing we were from Colorado, he told us he traveled frequently to Colorado, also a big sugar beet state. Specifically, he stayed in Greeley which he called the Wild West and mentioned how many people carried sidearms out in the open. I said, "Welcome to America."

We landed on time at almost midnight. As we made our way along the off-ramp, a tall, slick-looking dude in a black suit was holding up a sign that said, Welcome Browns. With his well-trimmed mustache, he reminded me of a young Omar Sharif. He was our greeter that our hotel had arranged to meet us at the airport.

With a big smile and slicked-back hair, Abdul led us through the modern, but very quiet airport to customs through which he ushered us in no time at all. And then Abdul led us to our luggage which had already gone through customs.

I thought, "Hey, this isn't bad. Egypt appeared to be efficient."

Abdul loaded our luggage onto a cart and led us outside to a Kempinski Nile Hotel van that was waiting for us. He then bid us goodbye. I was surprised. I had thought he would accompany us to the hotel but no. The driver of the van would do that. So I peeled off about five bucks worth of LEs for a tip and bid him goodbye. Abdul pocketed it with a big smile, probably indicating that it was too much for his services. In addition, I had already paid a hundred bucks for this airport greeting and drive to the hotel.

The thirty kilometer ride to the hotel took about an hour because even at this ungodly hour, the expressways were flush with cars. Rush hour at one a.m. The driver who spoke a little English indicated that this was normal. Along the way, we couldn't see much other than hulking, dark buildings that appeared to be apartment houses.

Eventually, we came into the interior streets of Cairo also full of traffic but eventually were on the drive along the Nile River, all lit up. Here the buildings were in the late stages of 19th-century elegance. Soon we were at our hotel, the Hotel Kempinski Nile. I tipped the driver, another couple of bucks in Egyptian pounds. (40 LE) Shit, I could see how the LEs could go fast here.

The entrance to the hotel was like a bunker with a narrow security entrance and armed guards along with a drug-sniffing dog. We went on through, placing our hand luggage onto an x-ray machine treadmill and soon were inside the hotel.

And what an inside it was--all marble with Art Deco Egyptian style images and hieroglyphs surrounding us. At the check-in desk, all was in order. We had a room on the third floor with a view of the Nile so said the clerk. As we made our way to the elevator I noticed that only males were on duty and that they were all dressed in black suits. Men in Black, anyone?

In no time we were in our room, once again tipping the porter a buck (20 LE). The clerk was right. From our balcony, we indeed had a view of the Nile. We got ready for bed, our heads still spinning from the turmoil of Cairo traffic and the trip in general. But soon we were sound asleep.

# 2. GIZA

**Sat. March 2**

Since the main Odyssey tour group was not arriving until late at night, Yvonne and I enjoyed a free day at the hotel, sleeping late, lounging around, and eating. The buffet breakfast was scrumptious with made to order omelets and a myriad of other goodies including exotic fruits. Later, I went swimming in the rooftop heated pool. It was like bathwater. The rooftop also offered great views of a very blue Nile with a multitude of bridges spanning its calm waters.

**Blue Nile**

*Africa: Around the Edges*

Looking at it, it was hard to imagine that the Nile was quite polluted with warnings never to swim in it. In addition, the rooftop offered great views of the surrounding buildings, many mansions home to various embassies.

**An Embassy?**

So we lounged around and at certain points enjoyed an adult beverage. For dinner, Yvonne didn't want to dress up and insisted on ordering room service. O.K. Fine. I nevertheless went down to the dining room and had Egyptian lasagna. It was not bad but certainly not Italian. Late that night, I heard banging around next door to us. I assumed it was somebody the main tour group settling in.

**Sun. March 3**

The next morning, I saw no sign of our Odyssey group in the breakfast room. I thought maybe they were sleeping in. In any case, I wanted to track down our tour leader. The concierge who knew all the Odyssey Egyptian tour directors directed me to one Doaa Foad sitting in the lobby alone on a couch. She was a 40ish looking woman with a headscarf. I walked over and introduced myself.

She replied in perfect English, "Ah, Mr. Brown I was wondering if you had arrived. I did note that you and your wife were not on the manifest of the tour group that flew in last night."

I explained that we had flown in early in order to recuperate from jet lag. She nodded saying she understood. She then told me we would have a group meeting at 10:00 a.m. to introduce ourselves and to discuss the tour. She also said, since our group arrived late, she decided to let them sleep late. As a result, we would have to forgo a half day of sightseeing. She explained that immediately following the meeting, we would go see the Giza Pyramids right outside of Cairo but not the Saqqara Step Pyramid as scheduled because it would be too much for one day. Doaa promised that we would see Saqqara when we returned to Cairo in ten days or so.

Looking at me, she said, "Be sure to bring some snacks from the breakfast room because we will have a very late lunch."

At our ten o'clock meeting, we met our fellow travelers, all twenty of them. Most were couples. All looked upper- middle class, mostly in their 60s. A few in their 70s and one gent, Mick, in his early 80s who was a live wire and self-proclaimed Washington insider. I could never figure out what he did other than escort important people around the Capitol which he let you know about. Later he told me he worked for the Carlyle group. He also had a sharp looking youngish wife, Debra.

One woman, Gloria, was an English professor at the Savannah School of the Art and Design. She was by herself and got on well with Yvonne. Then there were the Bobbsey Twins, two little Jewish guys in their 60s who were best friends and who were sharing a room. They told us that originally their wives had planned on coming along but bailed out at the last minute because of the terrorist threats. So they said to them,

"Screw it, we are still going."

And they did, leaving their wives at home.

Also in our group was a couple from Montecito, California. At one point I asked them if they had escaped the mudslides last year. They assured me that they had. There was also a high school teacher from the Bronx, a Jewish lady and her husband. We discussed the glories of living in New York. She also got along very well with Yvonne.

***

An hour later, we all boarded an Odyssey tour bus for a short ride to Giza. After battling our way through traffic for a half-hour, voila, there it was—Giza. Just like in the photos, the three big pyramids. The biggest being the Great Pyramid about 500-feet high built by Pharaoh Khufu around 2590 BC during the time of the Old Kingdom. All three pyramids were situated on a high plateau, scattered over several hundred yards. Today the wind was blowing hard kicking up dust with a lot of litter blowing around so it was difficult to make them out at first.

We were let off the bus and told by Doaa to wander around on our own. Good. Most of us hiked up to the Great Pyramid and examined this monstrous pile of limestone blocks up close. These babies weighed at least two and a half tons. Yvonne and I climbed up and over a few of these blocks but a guard was nearby so we didn't climb any higher. Just a couple of weeks ago, a Danish couple had climbed to the top of the Great Pyramid and allegedly had sex causing a big scandal. So now the guards were being extra vigilant.

**Great Pyramid**

**Building Blocks**

Then there was the tunnel issue, about a 150-meter long tunnel into the heart of the Great Pyramid that tourists could navigate. It was supposedly a mind-altering experience, something like communing with the ancients in their burial place. However, we had read that once inside there was nothing to see—no wall paintings, no mummies, no sarcophagi, nothing to do except to admire the stonework of tomb. You see, grave robbers got to this place a few centuries after the burial of the great Khufu.

Ultimately, we elected not to go into this tunnel because it was only four feet high for 100-meters before hitting the inner chamber. I am 6'2", Yvonne 5'9." Later a few in our group that did do the tunnel said wasn't worth it. Even Bruce, one of the little Jewish guys, said it wrecked his back, plus it was claustrophobic what with all the people crammed into the tunnel with nowhere to go. If somebody panicked, you were just shit out of luck.

We happily stayed outside and took photos and wandered around the other two lesser but still massive pyramids, the Pyramid of Khafre and the Pyramid of Menkaure. The peak of Khafre pyramid was still capped by a sheet of smooth, white limestone which once covered all the pyramids here.

*Africa: Around the Edges*

**Pyramid of Khafre**

Right near the Khafre pyramid was a pavilion that housed an ancient vessel called Solar Boat of the Pharaoh Khufu. (Note that Khufu was the father of Khafre.)

We entered the pavilion and were startled to see a full size, craft so large that we had to walk around it on a raised ramp in order to take it all in. It measured about 143- feet long and 20- feet wide. Dating from around 2500 BC, this boat was so well preserved that archeologists claimed that when reconstructed it could sail today on the Nile. This Solar Boat had been found buried in a sealed pit near the pyramid.

**Khufu Ship**

Following our view of the boat, we climbed aboard our tour bus and rode over to another pyramid viewing site. This was a site where we could see the classic view of all three pyramids lined up across the desert.

**The Big Three**

It was also an open, dusty area full of camel ride hustlers and tourist shops. The camels were a sorry looking bunch, old, scraggy and beaten down, nonetheless seemingly game to haul tourists around, of course, at the urging their handlers.

*Africa: Around the Edges*

**Camel Hustle**

Since both Yvonne and I had gone on extended camel rides in the Australian Outback years before, we didn't bother with the rides. But almost our entire group did and when they came back from their short fifteen-minute ride, they pronounced themselves thrilled.

As to the tourist trap shops, the hawkers were out in force proclaiming their wares. We tried to ignore them but they were persistent, not taking no for an answer and in your face all the time. Nonetheless, we smiled and moved on. However, later at the site of another tomb, I did yield and bought a head wrap similar to the dishrag that Yasser Arafat used to wear called a "keffiyeh." With my sunglasses on, I was told that I looked like a dangerous Middle Eastern dude.

After an hour or so of trudging around and snapping pictures, I began to wonder how the hell the ancient Egyptians ever built these pyramids.

There are many theories but the most popular one is that they dragged the two and a half ton blocks up ever higher on earthen ramps as the pyramid rose. That would require massive numbers of people to do that. Initially, archeologists thought they must have been slaves to perform this back-breaking work but the current theory is they were happy, well-paid workers doing this during their offseason when the Nile flooded. Indeed, there are many signs of extensive worker villages nearby these pyramids. However, the most intriguing theory to me is that the blocks were ferried to the pyramid base construction sites by a series of canals and then with air-filled skins for buoyancy strapped to them, the blocks were lifted into place by means of a water elevator, which is technically possible. Thus reducing the need for unlimited manpower. I wouldn't put it past these clever Egyptians.

Then there is the issue of the remote period for the construction of these pyramids which were among the most ancient monuments that we were going to see on this trip. Just imagine, the first were constructed roughly 4600 years ago or if you prefer 2600 years before the birth of Christ (BC) or more politically correct, 2600 years before the Common Era (BCE). I will use the BC designation throughout this account of our tour of Egypt.

So what was going on 46-hundred years ago? In addition to Egypt and its Nile, this was a time of other river civilizations such as the Assyrian civilization along the Tigris and the Euphrates rivers and in China, along the Yangtze River. It was a time of agricultural abundance over-seen by complex hierarchical societies, the top of which were invariably priests and divine rulers. Such it was in Egypt. Of course, there are endless arguments about which civilization preceded the other when it comes to Egypt and Assyria. But no matter. You get the idea. It was all a long, long time ago, hundreds of centuries ago. Unimaginable to most people, especially to the uninformed many of whom claim the earth is only 6-thousand years old and perhaps it was ancient aliens that built the pyramids.

For all the particulars about the emergence of ancient Egypt civilization, I offer my version of a simplified timeline in the appendix at the end of this account.

\*\*\*

Next, it was over to the Sphinx about a kilometer away from the main pyramids. At first, I thought we were going to walk over but no, we bussed it instead. Once we parked, Doaa was hustling people to follow her out into the Sphinx grounds, but at this point, I had another urgent mission. Luckily I had spotted a WC coming into this area so I hustled over to do my duty.

This was my first encounter with an Egyptian public toilet and I feared that the toilet would be nothing more than a hole in the ground over which you are supposed to squat. But, no. The restroom was relatively clean and there were regular flush toilets in the stalls. Still, there was no toilet paper, only a little man at the entrance who had several rolls that he would tear off for a price. But I outfoxed him since I had brought my own wipes along as per the recommendations of many Egyptian travelers. I thus successfully concluded my mission.

By the time I got out of the WC, my group was long gone in the distance. So I resolved to see the Sphinx on my own which was only about 200-meters away. As I started to trudge over, a young bearded dude came up to me and claimed that he was a tour guide and offered to show me a way to get the best shots of the Sphinx. Since there appeared to be a multitude of ways to get over there, I yielded and he proceeded to take me to a number of prime spots for taking photos. I gave him a buck in ELs for his troubles which he seemed happy with. By the way, I did manage to take some great shots of the Sphinx and thanks to my little zoom lens on my Canon point and shoot camera.

**Great Sphinx**

As is well known, the Sphinx is a weird looking lion-like creature with the face of a man and the body of a lion. Some Egyptologist say the face was modeled after the Pharaoh Khafre during the time of the Old Kingdom. Of course, the nose of the face had long since rotted away or possibly was shot off by Napoleon's troops for target practice in their 1778 expedition to Egypt.

Following this, I hiked back to the main entrance just in time to catch up with the group. I got several blank looks from my fellow group members and a frown from Doaa. But no worries, we climbed back on the bus and then proceeded to drive over to a nearby restaurant that had stunning long distance views of the Sphinx. There we indulged ourselves in a late lunch of lamb and various other Egyptian goodies with my favorite Egyptian beer, Stella Beer, to wash it down.

Later, back at our hotel, we went out again for dinner around eight. This time at the Blue Nile Restaurant situated right on the Nile. Good food, very picturesque what with the bridges and lights on the Nile. After that we were done, stuffed. Two big meals in one day, whew. Back at the hotel, we hit the sack early because tomorrow we would fly down to Aswan to see many more monuments of ancient Egypt.

# 3. PHILAE

**Mon. March 4**

Early the next morning, we flew to Aswan, about an hour flight over the desert some 860 kilometers from Cairo. This was the beginning of our excursion through Upper Egypt. It is important to keep in mind that Upper Egypt, while higher in elevation than Lower Egypt, it is really southern Egypt and Lower Egypt is actually northern Egypt. Further confusing the situation is that the Nile is a river that runs south to the north and into the Mediterranean. So the Upper Nile is really the southern Nile and the Lower Nile is really the northern Nile. Is that clear to everyone?

We won't even get into the issue of cataracts where you have to deal with references to the 1st, 2nd, and 3rd cataracts. Cataracts are simply another name for various rapid points along the Nile, most of which have disappeared because of the Aswan Dam.

Once off the plane, we were hustled over to a waiting tour bus and we immediately noticed the tight security everywhere along the road that was to take us to the Aswan Dam and to our first major site in Upper Egypt, the Temple of Philae. At a couple of checkpoints, we spotted armed troops toting what looked like AK-47s. Doaa explained that since this area was a military zone, security was extra tight.

**Checkpoint**

Anyway, we continued on to Philae but before we got there, we had to drive across the Aswan Dam and thereby had a great view of the dam and Lake Nasser, the lake that resulted from the damming of the Nile.

**Aswan Dam**

To me, the dam was not that impressive. Although about four kilometers long, it appeared to be a standard earth embankment dam, nothing as spectacular as the Grand Coulee Dam in Washington State. It was merely a low level, rock-filled dam with the lake on the south side and a modest-looking Nile river feeding out of it on the north side. No sheer concrete walls with dramatic spillways that you see on Shasta Dam in Northern California or for that matter, Hoover Dam in Nevada. Still, the Aswan Dam has an impressive history.

Built primarily by the Russians in the early 1960s during the rule of Gamal-Abdel Nasser, it was a massive construction project and it effectively modernized old-world Egypt with new electrical output and controlled irrigation. It also effectively ended the annual flooding of the Nile, a cycle upon which the ancient Egyptian civilization was based.

I remember reading about it in my Weekly Reader while in high school. While it appeared that the Russians did a good job of helping the Egyptians build the dam, the Russian electrical power generating facility only lasted a few years before it broke down. It was then the U.S. intervened and set up its own power generating facility which is still functioning today, although with modifications.

At the time there was a lot of controversy because as Lake Nasser began to fill up, the waters threatened many important ancient sites. Thus in the late 1960s, with a lot of international help and money, the Egyptians began to dismantle these ancient sites and re-assemble them on much higher ground.

The Temple of Philae was one of those moved to a higher elevation. In fact, as were to soon see, it was moved to a little island in the lake. How the Egyptians did this was a complicated process of breaking down the stone works and re-assembling them something like re-assembling a giant jigsaw puzzle. Later, we were to see a couple of films that would go into detail on this process.

Continuing to the jumping-off point to Philae Island, we parked in a lot full of buses and just beyond a beehive of tourist hutches replete with long-robed Egyptians touting their wares, sometimes right in your face. Our fearless guide Doaa brushed right through them leading us to a dock of sorts that was jammed with thirty-foot watercraft one of which would take us to the island site of Philae. The docking scene was utter chaos, as each boat seemed to take delight in jamming and bashing one another in order to gain a spot on the dock and thus have access to passengers.

**Boat Chaos**

At first, I thought this jamming was only accidental, but after a few seconds of observation, it was indeed intentional as the boat pilots goosed their outboards propelling their crafts into another, all with a big smile on their faces. Welcome to the chaos that is Egypt, they seemed to say.

Eventually, we did all board the same boat and got underway for a short ride to Philae Island. Our disembarkation was much more orderly at the Philae dock and we obediently followed Doaa up a path that led to the much-admired main temple of Philae. Actually, Philae Island was comprised of several temples in addition to this main temple dedicated to Isis which you see on all the tourist posters.

*Africa: Around the Edges*

**Temple of Philae**

It should be noted that the temples of Philae are not that old in terms of the ancient Egypt of 2600 BC. The earliest surviving temple buildings at Philae date from around 370 BC under the reign of Ptolemy II and later under the rule of several Roman Emperors into the ADs.

Since the Ptolemies were essentially Greek rulers of Egypt for about three centuries from about 305 BC until 30 BC, they made every effort to integrate themselves into Egyptian culture with all the symbolism, historical and religious references to its ancient past. So it was that this temple in this complex was dedicated to the Egyptian goddess Isis. It was also said to be one of the burying places of the Osiris, the Egyptian god of the dead, the underworld and resurrection.

To cover it all, Doaa led us from one area of the temple to another expounding on one wall relief or inscription after another. I soon became bored with that and headed off on my own snapping photos with my Canon camera.

Oh, I should mention I wasn't wearing my "whisperer" at any time. These whisperers were little wireless contraptions with an earpiece that were tuned to Doaa's narration via a little microphone headset that she wore. I found them extremely annoying and awkward to use so I immediately dispensed with them. Instead, if I wanted to hear what she was saying I would simply get within earshot of her. If I was off wandering around on my own and wanted any hard information on what I was seeing, I would refer to my Lonely Planet guide to Egypt.

Thence, I made my way over another area of the island where I encountered the Gateway of Hadrian and gazed at this rather impressive temple with flavors of Roman and Greek architecture. Hadrian was a Roman Emperor in the 2nd century AD.

**Hadrian Gate**

As I looked about, I had to keep reminding myself again that what I was seeing here was a reconstruction of a temple removed from its original site. Add to that it was the fact that all these so-called ancient temples here were the product of the Ptolemies' imagination of what ancient Egypt must have been like a thousand or so years before their arrival.

Or as Jason Thompson puts it in his one-volume History of Egypt:

*"Much of our impression of what ancient Egyptian temples were like come from the Ptolemys because the remaining ancient temples that are most intact were built by the Ptolemys such as Dendera, Edfu, Kom Ombo and above all, beautiful Philae."*

So, the question has to be asked: Just how authentic was this site and the many others like it that we were scheduled to visit? I sensed that these Ptolemy reconstruction sites might be on the order of very sophisticated Disney World attractions, even though they were blessed and authenticated by many Egyptologists.

After a couple of hours or so on the Philae Island, it was back to the boat for a ride to the docks and there amid, much more bashing and crashing into other boats, we disembarked, made our way through the hordes of screaming merchants touting their wares and into our nice air-conditioned bus.

Moments later were arrived at the dock where our Lake Nasser vessel, the Omar El Khayam was moored and which was to transport us for the next several days to one monument after another. As we were to discover, Omar El Khayam was not a super luxurious vessel, in fact, a little dated, but it was comfortable and well suited to the cruising job for which it was intended.

Immediately upon boarding the boat, it weighed anchor and we were off. A half-hour at the bar discussing our day's adventure was followed by a good dinner and then it was an early evening crash to end our first long day in Upper Egypt.

**Omar El Khayam**

# 4. KALABSHA

**Tue. March 5**

The following morning we woke up at our next temple site, the temple of Kalabsha, a Nubian built temple dedicated to the Nubian god Mandulis who was a lower form of Horus as a symbol of kingship.

Kalabsha was built during the Roman period around 30 BC. The relocated temple itself was way off in the distance on a hilltop, so a ride was offered in the form of a tractor pulling a trailer. Feeling feisty and in need of some morning exercise, about half of the group set off on foot to cover the kilometer distance to the temple. The rest of us lazy slogs climbed aboard the tractor-trailer and relaxed as it bumped along. But feeling guilty, I did jump off at one point and dashed up a steep short cut to the temple, thereby getting my dose of morning exercise.

This temple was indeed an impressive sight from a distance with its two towering pylons flanking the entrance.

**Kalabsha Temple**

But when I entered it, it struck me as rather dull. There were a couple of reliefs of interest including one of the god Horus emerging from reeds. (Moses legend anyone?) And a Roman inscription forbidding pigs in the temple. Best of all, the temple situated on a hilltop offered great views of the countryside and Lake Nasser.

**Lake Nasser**

However, we spent little time here and were hustled back to the boat for our next site, the nearby temple of Beit El-Wali.

**Beit El-Wali**

*Africa: Around the Edges*

    Like Philae, this rock-cut temple had been moved to higher ground to avoid the waters of Lake Nasser. But unlike Philae, this temple was an original to its time of Ramses II (c.1250 BC). In fact, he was the one who had it built. Beit El-Wali was dedicated to the deities of Amun-Re (Sun God), Khnum and Anuket (god & goddess of the Nile)

    The most attractive feature of this temple was a series of color interior wall paintings pretty much intact. Here I saw Ramses II being suckled by Anuket and later in life Ramses II smiting an enemy of Egypt.

**Ramses II Being Nursed**

**Ramses II Smiting an Enemy**

I snapped away at these almost perfectly preserved color images. I felt like I could reach out and touch these long-departed ancients marveling how vibrant and lifelike their images were after some 32-hundred years of history.

Following our visit to Beit El-Wali, that was it for the day. We returned to the ship for an afternoon of leisure and later, a dinner. All was well as the Omar El Khayam weighed anchor and made for our next destination.

# 5. TEMPLES GALORE

**Wed. March 6**

Overnight we floated along for a few more miles and in the early morning, we passed by a couple of humble huts situated out on a peninsula. It was hard to imagine anyone living in these tumbled abodes but most likely somebody did.

**Humble Hut**

Our first outing for the day was a visit to Wadi Al Sabu also known at the Valley of the Lions and to several other temples all located within walking distance of each other. But to keep things moving along, Doaa had arranged a donkey transportation cart for those who did not want to walk much.

**Donkey Cart**

First up was the temple of Amun of Ramses II even though most of it had been built centuries later during the reign of the Ptolemies. Still, the temple was impressive as we marched up the promenade and were greeted by a series of fearsome-looking lions/sphinxes and statues of Ramses II which were original to his time.

*Africa: Around the Edges*

**Ramses II Temple**

Interior to the temple we found more statues of Ramses II and a relief of him presenting an offering to the gods of Wadi es-Sebua.

**Offering to the Gods**

Moving along, we donkey carted it over to the Temple of Dakka dedicated to Thoth, the god of wisdom.

**Temple of Dakka**

Upon entering its interior, we found a series of well-preserved reliefs including one of the Kushite kings, Arkamani presenting an offering to the gods.

**Kushite King Arkamani**

*Africa: Around the Edges*

Following the Wadi es Sebua area, we rode over to the Temple of Amada (c. 1479 BC). This was truly an original ancient temple constructed centuries well before the time of the Ptolemies. It too had been moved here intact from its original site in order to escape the rising waters of Lake Nasser.

**Temple of Amada**

The Temple of Amada was dedicated to Amenhotep II, (c. 1427 BC) who was no slouch himself having been a warrior first-class conquering many threatening tribes and expanding the Egyptian empire. From the outside, this temple wasn't much to look at but inside it was a treasure trove of colorful reliefs. One particular relief described how Amenhotep II hung six rebel chiefs from Syria.

**Interior Amada**

Done with Amada, we climbed back on the donkey cart and down the path, we passed by a couple of Nubian dwellings which offered us a view into their unique architecture featuring beehive-like rounded cupulas.

**Nubian Dwellings**

*Africa: Around the Edges*

I should also mention that our driver was a classic looking Nubian himself, probably resembling the Nubians of ancient times. I couldn't resist and asked him for permission to take a photo, for a price of course.

**Our Nubian Driver**

Next up on this day chock full of temples, we took a look at the Temple of Derr, a rock-cut Egyptian temple built by the ever ubiquitous Ramses II early in his 60-year reign. Like most of the other temples in these parts, the Temple of Derr was dismantled in the 1960s and re-assembled here.

**Temple of Derr**

The Temple of Derr's chief attraction was the unusually bright colors of its reliefs depicting all manner of homage being paid to Ramses II.

**Homage to Ramses II**

By this time, we realized that we had seen all of this before or reliefs very much like it. This is because the ancient Egyptians had no qualms about copying the same ceremonial images over and over while depicting various scenes with various rulers. Add to that the fact that all these images are rendered in a flat two-dimensional style with everybody in profile. To me, it was all becoming rather static and monotonous after a while.

After perusing the Derr temple, we remounted the Nubians donkey train which ferried our sorry tired asses back to the Omar El Khayam for rest and recuperation. Next up tomorrow, the big Kahuna of ancient Egyptian monuments, Abu Simbel.

# 6. ABU SIMBEL

**Wed. March 7**

It wasn't much of float down to our next site, only a few miles overnight. But when we awoke, we were greeted with an awesome sight even at a distance—Abu Simbel!

**Abu Simbel**

Abu Simbel (1264 BC) was by far the largest monument that we had seen yet dedicated to Ramses II. This guy was like catshit. His monuments are everywhere. However, there is a debate about how great he really was. Early in his reign, he went to war with the Hittites in an area now known as Syria. It was a major battle, the Battle of Kadesh (1274 BC) with thousands dead on each side. Essentially it was a draw but not to Ramses II who declared it a tactical victory on his side and propagandized about his great feat incessantly both in recorded hieroglyphic history and in pictorial reliefs.

In any case, he reigned for over sixty years (1279-1213 BC), engaged in many other battles and enlarged his kingdom. The Abu Simbel monument marks the most southern part of his conquest in Upper Egypt, taking over what was then northern Nubia.

So how did we handle this iconic monument? First, our little transit boat docked at a tourist village, obviously set up to fleece the tourists as they set about hiking over to the monument. Ignoring the throngs of merchants hawking their wares, we trudged along a well-trodden dirt road leading up to the monument. As we did so, I took a good look at the backside of the hill that the monument was housed in. Yes housed. I will explain.

You see Abu Simbel was also relocated from its original site due to the rising waters of Lake Nasser. As we saw later in a movie short at the tourist center, it was a massive project, tearing it down block by block, numbering and categorizing each block and then re-assembling the blocks and statues like a giant jigsaw puzzle as I have noted before. It took years in the late 60s and early 70s to do this. In order to give the monument a setting appropriate to its original setting, the Egyptians built an artificial hill into which to insert the monument. That was what I was seeing now, noting that the hill did indeed looked artificial.

**Fake Hill**

No matter, what counted was how the monument itself looked. When we arrived at its base moments later, it did indeed look like it had been here forever with its iconic four statues of Ramses II out front staring us down throughout the centuries.

**Abu Simbel Statues**

*Africa: Around the Edges*

These babies were monsters, twenty meters high, (c. 72-feet). You can also see that the second one from the left has no head. It was damaged by an earthquake. The head and the torso can be seen at the statue's feet. All these statues were sculpted from the rock of the original site.

After wandering around the outside for a while being duly impressed by their magnificence, we went inside to exam its interior marvels. The only catch being no photographs were allowed inside this hallowed monument unless you bought a photo pass for about 300 LE (about 17-dollars). A price I thought outrageous at the time since I had been happily snapping interior photos at other monuments for zip. I will have much more to say about the no-photography racket at these monuments later in this account. Nonetheless, the following is a stock photo of the interior.

**Interior Abu Simbel**

Of course, when we went in, we found the interior was gloomy and less impressive. Amazing what good lighting can do.

Onward. After twenty minutes or so of focusing on this Ramses II monument of Abu Simbel, we hiked over to a lesser monument dedicated to Ramses' first wife, Nefertari. Do not confuse Nefertari with an earlier Egyptian princess, the famous Nefertiti from around 1350 BC.

**Nefertari Monument**

Nefertari was a beauty herself and it is important to note of the many later wives and mistresses of Ramses II only Nefertari was immortalized in a monument of her own dedicated to the goddess of Hathor. It might be also worth knowing that Nefertari was said to be of Nubian descent, i.e. black but in all the depictions we saw of her, she was light brown like most of the royal Egyptians.

Again, no interior photos unless you paid up. So while we did explore the interior of the Nefertari monument, you will have to settle for this stock shot.

**Interior Nefertari Monument**

After exploring this monument, Yvonne and I milled around with the others for a while, taking more photos but then growing bored, we decided to trek back to the visitor center where we watched the movie on the relocation of Abu Simbel.

Following that we made our way back through the crowd of screaming vendors and returned to the tender boat eventually meeting up with the others. We boarded the tender and chugged our way back to the Omar El Khayam.

Oh, I forgot. One persistent vendor did manage to convince Yvonne to buy a beautiful small woven rug from him that he insisted was unique and all for a modest price. So she bit and bought it. Of course, later at other tourist locations, we saw the very same rug on sale. It turned out to be a ubiquitous tourist item. Yvonne said she didn't care since it was still a nice throw rug. O.K.

Guess what? Since there were no other scheduled sights to see on this day, we chilled on the Omar El Khayam for the afternoon. At one point, I went up on the top deck and took a plunge into their ice-cold swimming pool. Luckily it was offset by a warm sun which I took advantage of trying to get an early start on my tan. Of course, I was aided by a cool Stella beer.

Maybe it was too much sun because I was zonked out by late afternoon and all I wanted to do was eat dinner and go to bed early. Yvonne felt the same way. But wait.

We were supposed to go back over to Abu Simbel after dark for a light and sound program on the wonders of Abu Simbel but we had heard that the program was hokey so we took a pass. Later, we could hear the dramatic music issuing forth over the waters of the lake and could see in the distance the images flashing up on the monuments. Good enough for us. We just retired early.

# 7. ASWAN

**Fri. March 8**

The next morning, a few of the people who had gone to the sound and light show acknowledged that it had been pretty bad. No big loss. Around nine, we left the good ship Omar El Khayam and boarded a bus for a three-hour drive back to Aswan.

This was an interesting drive because we could see Egypt more close up than floating by it on a luxury boat. First, we passed through the town of Ambu Simbel itself located on the artificial peninsula built from the mainland out to the Abu Simbel Island. This town was the result of the thousands who had worked on the re-assembly of the monument. It appeared to be a nice little town, neat and clean unlike most of the towns we were to see in Egypt.

**Town of Abu Simbel**

Once out of the peninsula, we hit the real countryside which except for some scanty palm trees and various bushes rapidly turned into a stark brown desert. Not a sandy desert, more like a dirt desert. However, it still held our interest to see what the real Egypt looked like as we passed by one forlorn looking dwelling after another. Eventually, outside of a more prosperous looking town, we crossed a canal which Doaa said had been recently built under the direction of Egyptian President El-Sisi. It was all part of a wide-ranging plan to irrigate the desert and make it bloom.

**New Canal**

According to Doaa, El-Sisi had other big plans as well for Egypt such as improving the infrastructure of cities, in fact, building new towns altogether. Even now a new administrative center for the Egyptian government was under construction as well as other new cities strategically placed around Egypt. The main goal of these new cities was to reduce the population of Cairo's some 22-million with the lure of better housing and better job opportunities.

As we moved on, in addition to the spanking new canal, we could see signs of new electrical power grids, more irrigation, flourishing crops, and much-improved roads.

*Africa: Around the Edges*

On the negative side, I did notice about every thirty to fifty kilometers or so, we had to pass through heavily guarded and armed checkpoints. Military types with automatic rifles and even an armored vehicle with a manned machine gun in the turret.

**Checkpoint**

For us, it was not a problem being on a tourist bus. We would whiz right through, but if you were traveling in a private car you were stopped and questioned, no doubt required to show your papers, etc. All quite scary. But then what terrorist in their right mind would ever strike at a well-known checkpoint?

Still, these terrorists never give up. While we were in Upper Egypt, the Egyptian authorities broke up a ring of terrorists in a bomb-making apartment in the Giza area of Cairo on March 7. It seems these would-be terrorists had disguised themselves as street custodians. The idea was to plant a bomb or an IUD, near or under a tourist bus. As it turned out, all were fatally shot as the police/army burst into the apartment. No time for judicial procedure in Egypt, I guess.

But enough of the dark side of Egypt for we soon arrived at the town of Aswan and went directly to the Nubian Museum. This was an impressive looking building, designed in the Nubian style and once inside, we found many fascinating exhibits, especially the sculptures of Nubian royalty.

**Nubian Museum**

In many ways, Nubia (also called the Kingdom of Kush) located in what is now northern Sudan and southern Egypt rivaled their Egyptian counterparts. First, their country was the source of Egypt's mineral wealth especially gold. Second, they were great warriors and at certain times in Egyptian history, they ran Egypt. There even were a few Nubian pharaohs (c. 744--656 BC).

*Africa: Around the Edges*

**Nubian Pharaoh Taharqa 690 BC**

However, for most of the ancient period, the Egyptians controlled Nubia and ran it as a client state. They also made full use of its fearsome Nubian warriors in their own Egyptian armies. Also, as we were seeing, the Nubians were very advanced in the arts of sculpting, pottery, fabric design, etc.

After perusing the museum's offerings for a while, I went back outside to the luxurious gardens surrounding the museum just in time to hear the noontime call to prayer issuing forth from a nearby mosque. Since it was Friday, the day of rest and prayer in Islam, I also heard a short sermon from the local Iman over the loudspeaker. Everybody around working in the garden and others nearby stopped what they were doing, did the prayer thing. Some had little prayer rugs with them on which to kneel. Others simply sat on a garden wall to listen to the Iman. I too sat on the wall and listened even though I couldn't understand a word of what was being said. Nonetheless, it was peaceful and enlightening seeing these people worship.

Soon, Doaa came out of the museum followed by the others and we boarded the bus and made our way over to the docks along the Nile. There we boarded our next ship for a couple of days of cruising the Nile. Like the Omar El Khayam, the Farah Nile was a comfortable river going vessel with a rooftop pool and bar.

Once settled and lunched, it was time for a felucca sail. These feluccas that still sail today up and down the Nile are modeled after the ancient ones. They are skinny, flat-bottomed boats with a wooden hull and triangular-shaped sails that are easily adjusted for changing winds and currents. When necessary, oars are used to power the felucca. They are specifically designed for protected river travel and not for open waters. As we were to see, they are indeed graceful looking as they scoot along.

**Feluccas on the Nile**

Our felucca was one of the bigger ones and all twenty of us were able to squeeze in. The boat was manned by a couple of Nubians who seemed to know what they were doing. So with a gust of breeze, we were off from the dock and soon sailing down the Nile for about a kilometer. Along the way, we passed Kitchener Island, a beautiful garden island in the middle of the Nile.

Do you remember your British colonial history? Lord Horatio Kitchener was the British Commander that reconquered Sudan in 1898 and who ultimately drowned during World War I when the British warship he was on sank. Unfortunately, we did not stop at Kitchener Island but merely sailed past it.

**Kitchener Island**

Overall, this short cruise was quite peaceful but towards the end, the hustle began. First, it was from a flotilla of paddleboards manned by youngsters who had paddled out onto the Nile, then clung to our sideboards and started begging for money.

**Little Beggar**

Then one of our Nubian sailors unveiled an array of tourist trinkets that he had squirreled away on the boat. One glance convinced me that it was all junk but our ever-accommodating fellow passengers did buy various trinkets that I was sure would end up in a trash barrel at the airport.

Soon we were back on board the Farah Nile and minutes later the vessel weighed anchor. From the top deck, we watched the Nile shoreline unfold as if we were seeing it on a widescreen movie.

*Africa: Around the Edges*

**Nile Shoreline**

Dinner was a low key affair and soon we were all in our cabins sound asleep.

# 8. KOM OMBO

**Sat. March 9**

When we woke up the next morning, we were docked at the ancient trading town of Kom Ombo. Our first major outing was to the Nubian Temple of Kom Ombo which was a well- preserved temple with little wear or tear from the Ptolemy period from around 332 BC. It was also unusual in that it was dedicated to two gods, Sobek, the crocodile god and Horus, the falcon-headed god.

**Kom Ombo Temple**

We didn't have far to go to get to this temple because we had docked only a 100-meters away. As we wandered around its massive columns, Yvonne took particular delight in this temple precisely because she identified with her favorite god Sobek which she considered her spiritual mentor in ancient Egypt.

**Kom Ombo Columns**

Often seen as a man with a crocodile head, Sobek's main job was to control the waters of the Nile and to protect the pharaoh from evil through its military prowess. He also had a hand in ensuring fertility. I liked Sobek too because his job was so clear cut and unlike many Egyptian gods, he didn't have multiple names and a confusing heritage.

Sobek

Following a look around at the temple, we hiked over to a museum that featured mummified crocodiles in honor of Sobek.

**Crocodile Museum**

Displayed along with the mummified crocs were crocodile eggs, crocodile statues, and crocodile sarcophagi. Also, the museum had a neat gift shop with artistically done crocodile figurines and beetle figures. We bought a scarab beetle paperweight since beetles figured big in Egyptian mythology too. In fact, the scarab beetle god, Khepri, was considered the god of creation and of the movement of the sun and rebirth. A rather full plate for an Egyptian god.

And that was our morning in Kom Ombo. We soon weighed anchor and headed downstream on the Nile for a couple of hours or so to the large agricultural town of Edfu  The major attraction here was the Temple of Edfu on the far edge of town but first, in order to get there, Doaa had arranged a caravan of horse-drawn carriages for our group.

**Carriage Transport**

O.K. I thought. Quaint, but why not? Yvonne and I climbed aboard our duly authorized carriage. The driver nodded, mumbled a few words of welcome in English and we were off with a bunch of other carriages trotting down the main boulevard of Edfu.

Along the way, we could see that many residents still wore the traditional Islamic garb of long robes called "galabeya." This was very common in the smaller Egyptian towns far from Cairo but in the more populated areas like Cairo about the only homage to Islam on the part of the woman was a headscarf (hijab). The rest of their garb was very often western with slacks, jeans, sneakers and tops often with brand names printed across.

**Edfu Women**

Overall, I had the feeling that modern Egyptian women and men paid only minimal attention to the dictates of Islam. Oh, many still did the call to prayer routine but many did not. After all, you have to remember that Islam was a religion forced upon Egypt by its Arab conquers in the 7th century AD. As a result, many Egyptians can take it or leave it despite what quasi-terrorist organizations like the Muslim Brotherhood insist on. Even Egyptian President El-Sisi has declared Egypt a secular state.

But hark! After trotting a couple of kilometers, we arrived at the Temple of Edfu. It was indeed a magnificent looking temple with towering pylons flanking its entrance but it was also another Ptolemy construct from around 237 BC and really all about the Hellenistic period of Egypt.

Once again it was more than obvious that during their three hundred year reign the Greek Ptolemies had made every effort to preserve the ancient Egyptian culture with all its priests and gods and to emulate their constructions and various statues, inscriptions and hieroglyphic messages. The Ptolemy goal in doing this was to promote stability in the country and profitability during their rule. Very enlightened rulers I would say. Of course, it all ended badly in 30 BC when Cleopatra, the last Ptolemy ruler committed suicide and the Romans took over control of Egypt and henceforth used it as a breadbasket and a taxing resource.

**Temple of Edfu**

But I digress. We entered as a group and started looking around at the statues and inscriptions. I hung with the group for a while and listened to Doaa describing various aspects of the temple, especially her detailed analysis of the many reliefs on its walls and pylons. But, alas, soon I grew bored with her recitation and went off on my own to explore the various chambers of this intricate and maze-like temple.

By and by, I found myself all alone in one of the many isolated back chambers. This one had reliefs galore engraved on its walls. As I studied the various depictions of the different gods and goddesses as well as the scenes of everyday routine, I suddenly had an eerie feeling of being teletransported back to those ancient times.

**Edfu Relief**

I stood there stupefied for several minutes, yet soaking up the images almost rendering them life-like in my mind. Soon I felt so remote from the 21st-century world that I felt I had entered another dimension. Finally, I turned away, hustled out of that inner chamber and went back outside. Near the main entrance, I sat on a broken down pillar and collected my wits as I waited for others from the group to emerge.

I waited and waited but no one showed up. Shit, I thought, I must have missed them. So I backtracked to the area where I had left them earlier. No one. Then I thought surely I would be able to spot them coming back through the main entrance. Maybe they were just taking longer than the allotted time.

However, when I returned to the main entrance, still no sign of the group. I decided, fuck it, I'm getting out of here. If I have to take a taxi back to the boat, so be it. But just as I was making my way out the temple complex to the street, two Egyptian cops came hustling up to me with Doaa in tow.

"Mr. Brown. We lost you. We have been waiting for a half-hour for you to show up. As you can see, I even sent the police to look for you," she scolded.

"Well, sorry for the trouble," I replied. "But I did wait for you at the main entrance for about a half-hour."

"Oh, well you see, I took the group out of the temple through a side entrance that was much shorter and less crowded."

"Oops. Sorry again."

And with that, she led me to the group which was climbing aboard those same horse-drawn carriages that had brought us here. Yvonne and I located our carriage and climbed on board. Of course, on the way back I had to endure Yvonne scolding me for causing so much trouble. At that point, I didn't care. I had had my moment of communion with the Egyptian ancients.

Twenty minutes later we were back at the boat and the driver started making noises that he wanted a generous tip. I tipped him the equivalent of two bucks. He sneered at that and then said, "What about my horse?"

I yielded and gave him one buck for the horse and then bid him goodbye and good riddance.

***

Later at dinner, Doaa held an Egyptian Night. The idea was that we were to dress up as Egyptians. A few of the women managed with their recently purchased glittery tourist junk and make-shift Egyptian gowns but most of the men did nothing but wear the traditional red fez. I was male the hit of the party because I was wearing my Arafat headpiece with the excess material draped around my shoulders over a Hawaiian shirt. I then topped it off with my large sunglasses which made me look like a real Middle Eastern thug. Everybody got a big laugh out of that. After downing a few wanna-be Margaritas and dinner, everybody retired to their cabins. The Farah Nile then weighed anchor and began our overnight cruise down the Nile to our next stop: Luxor and the Karnak Temple.

# 9. LUXOR

**Sun. March 10**

Come morning, we were tied up at the Luxor waterfront. We had our usual buffet breakfast of made-to-order omelets with many strange sausages and potato things, much fruit and other goodies all the while trying to relax. I was beginning to feel templed out. Yvonne not so much. But the one of the most legendary awaited—Karnak featuring the ever-present Ramses II.

Yvonne and I were eating alone for a change having grown tired of the constant socializing of our group. I mean they were all nice people. No real assholes in the bunch. Yvonne and I were not used to such constant socializing. We needed some alone time at our breakfast.

Still, we could not escape the buzz which was at high volume this morning. Everybody was so excited at the prospect of seeing one of the most spectacular ancient monuments in Egypt. Karnak. This was no Ptolemy re-construct. This monument spread over forty acres was the real McCoy dating originally from 2055 BC, the beginning of the Middle Kingdom and then added to and reconstructed up through the reign of Ramses II during the New Kingdom (1550-1069 BC)

**Avenue of Lions**

By nine o'clock, we were all gathered along the Avenue of Lions leading to the megalithic pylons of Karnak way off in the distance. As we approached, the entrance pylons grew larger and larger in our view as we grew smaller and smaller, like insignificant insects. I guess that was the idea to make us mere mortals feel puny in the sight of the Pharaoh gods.

Once inside the entrance, we made our way through the Great Hypostyle Hall with its towering 30-meter high pillars, still feeling like insects and then through other pylons to various inner courtyards too numerous to count.

*Africa: Around the Edges*

**Great Hypostyle Hall**

Karnak was comprised of many parts, not only of the Great Hypostyle Hall but also the temples of Amun, Mut and Motu. It seemed like it went on forever as we plodded from one section to another. Of course, one of the more impressive sights was the 30-meter obelisk standing alone and dedicated to Queen Hatshepsut (1473 -1458 BC)

**Hatshepsut Obelisk**

As we were to discover, Karnak was mainly an outdoor monument. In our time there we saw few interior chambers. Most of the inscriptions and reliefs we saw were on walls and columns. Of course, Karnak was replete with scores of statues mainly of Ramses II even though many other pharaohs contributed to Karnak.

In the end, after a couple of hot, sweaty hours in the beating down sun with Doaa droning on, we pooped out even though we had seen only a fraction of what Karnak had to offer. One could spend days here and still not get through it.

Following Karnak, we bussed it over to a so-called papyrus museum which was really only a tourist shop dedicated to selling various papyrus products.

However, the fellows who ran it did demonstrate how papyrus was made from the papyrus plant. Basically, it involved stripping the long papyrus plant stem, cutting it up into slices, and then soaking the slices in water.

**Papyrus Making**

Following that, the papyrus slices would be pounded and then rolled into flat slices. After aligning the flat slices on a cloth, a press machine would then flatten them out even more and at the same time blend them into sheets that would eventually become writable papyrus.

All very instructive and one of the reasons the Egyptian civilization even existed and flourished. They had something upon which to record their doings that was easily manageable. Not like the Assyrians who initially used clay tablets and stone stele to record the doings of their civilization in a rather cumbersome way.

Following the museum, we returned to the Farah Nile for lunch and a bit of a chill. On the afternoon docket was a visit to the Luxor Temple which was right in the center of town and following that a visit to the premier open-air tourist market in Luxor.

The problem was after a Stella beer and a full lunch, I wasn't in the mood to go see another temple no matter how important it was. Let alone a tourist market. What I did do was hand over my little Canon camera to Yvonne who was still game to see Luxor and told her to take some good shots. So off she went with the others while I hunkered down in my cabin and had a snooze.

Much later, when she returned exhausted from the sightseeing, the market and the heat, she handed over the camera, saying, "Take it, Allan. It was the best I could do. Anyway, you were right. Luxor was one temple too many for today. It seemed to me to be just a smaller Karnak. Probably a lot more than that but I couldn't pay that much attention. The market was a bust as well. Typical tourist junk."

**Luxor Temple**

Yvonne did manage to take some good shots of Luxor Temple and I complimented her for her photo savvy.

To cap off our day, we went up to the top deck of the ship to watch the sinking sun and had a cocktail. Then we descended to dinner. Following dinner, there was supposed be belly dancing entertainment, but I went back to our cabin to read. Yvonne stayed on. She later told me the belly dancer was grossly fat and not much to look at. So much for our first day in Luxor. Tomorrow the much-touted Valley of Kings.

# 10. VALLEY OF THE KINGS

**Mon. March 11**

The first thing we did in the morning was to pack up and say goodbye to the Farah Nile. Our luggage was going over to the Steigenberger Luxor Palace Hotel where we would be staying the night. We were done with cruising the Nile. From here on our tour would be land-based. Of course, as mentioned before the big activity for the day was to tour the Valley of the Kings a few kilometers west of Luxor and nowhere near the Nile.

Yvonne and I had done a fair amount of reading and video watching about the Valley of the Kings before the trip. It seems the pharaohs were tired of seeing the treasures of their pyramid tomb predecessors being ripped off by tomb robbers. Around 1600 BC during the New Kingdom, the pharaohs abandoned pyramid building and started burrowing into the hillsides of a desert valley and constructing their tombs, elaborate tombs as we would see.

Once again, we dutifully climbed aboard our tour bus and settled back for about a half-hour ride to the site. I should mention here that I had come down with a cold a couple of days ago and wasn't feeling too energetic but hey, I wasn't going to miss this.

As we approached the valley, I noted that the surrounding hills were rather barren with little or no vegetation. I had imagined craggy hills with some vegetation or at least towering sand dunes but no. What I saw were dirt hills like something you might see in a major construction site in its preliminary phase. In other words, I didn't think the Valley of the Kings was a very scenic place in which to entomb Egyptian royalty.

**Valley of the Kings**

Once parked in the vast parking lot, we piled off the bus and made our way through the standard tourist market with the merchants touting their wares, sometimes right into your face. Past the market, we gathered around the ticket office while Doaa collected our tickets to see the tombs. She then announced that if we wanted to see the King Tut tomb we would have to pay extra, another five bucks or so.

At the same time, she warned that photos were not allowed in there. If you wanted to photograph any of the other tomb interiors, you had to pay a photo fee of around twelve dollars. This in addition to the normal entrance fee which Doaa had covered. What a racket I thought but I still coughed up the extra bucks for both the Tut tomb and for the privilege of photographing inside the other tombs. Yvonne said she didn't care about the Tut tomb. I could go in alone.

Thus it was we hiked up the hill to the entrances of the main tombs. First up was the tomb of the sons of Ramses II and many sons there were. This was the most extensive tomb in the valley, in essence, a family mausoleum. Following that, we went in and looked around inside the tomb of Ramses VI. It had been recommended by Doaa as being one of the most decorated. And indeed it was as I snapped away.

**Ramses VI Tomb**

For the record, the carved decorations told of the afterlife of the king connecting him to the sun god Ra and with Orsis but there was no sarcophagus of Ramses VI. Apparently, his mummified body now resides in the Cairo Museum. Next up for me was the King Tut tomb. I was anxious to get in there before it was overwhelmed with crowds.

**King Tut Tomb**

Alas, there was not much to see. The restored burial chamber was small and had only modest decorations showing Tut being greeted by the gods Osiris and Mut, a mother goddess, but it did have a glass sealed sarcophagus in which lay the mummy of King Tut with his golden mask. I couldn't resist. Despite the prohibition, I proceeded to snap off a few pictures of Tut over the screaming protests of the few people who were already in there. I simply shrugged and got out of the tomb quick. Luckily, there was no Egyptian official around to confiscate my camera.

**King Tut Sarcophagus**

Let's pause for a moment here and discuss the King Tut-mania. The main reason so much is made of this boy king who ruled for only eleven years (1332-23 BC) was that archeologist Howard Carter discovered his tomb intact in 1922. Grave robbers had never touched it and it was full of fantastic treasures. It was also a perfect example of what artifacts Egyptian pharaohs were buried with to make their afterlife more comfortable.

However, King Tutankhamen didn't last that long. He reigned for the eleven years to the age of 18 when he died a mysterious death. Of much more interest historically was his father Akhenaten who established a new religion and new supreme god, the sun god Aten and a new Egyptian capital in Amarna. Further, Akhenaten's wife and Tut's probable mother was the beautiful Nefertiti a bust of which we saw a few years ago in the Pergamon Museum in Berlin.

**Queen Nefertiti**

When Akhenaten died, also somewhat mysteriously, the boy Tut took over as pharaoh, but it was his Grand Visier Ay who called the shots until Tut hit his teenage years and summarily fired Ay as Grand Visier. Tut then ruled, restored the old religions and engaged in battle until he was wounded in the leg which became infected and he forthwith died.

We poked around a couple more tombs and then after a couple of hours or so returned to the bus in the burning heat. Once again we had to pass through the market but this time the hustlers got me. I was very thirsty and out of energy so I bought a cold bottle of Coca Cola from a vendor with a cooler strategically placed at the entrance of the souk. It was a rip-off. About four dollars a bottle but I didn't care. I gulped it down like a pig, all to myself while Yvonne was off perusing the offerings at the various stalls.

Next up was the temple of the pharaoh queen Hatshepsut (1473-58 BC) also known as Deir el-Bahri. It was about a kilometer away so course we bussed it over. Good thing too because by now it was blazing hot. Once parked, we hiked up a long plaza all the time keeping this temple in view. From afar, I thought we were looking at some Nazi construct by Nazi architect Albert Speer.

**Temple Deir el-Bahri**

As Yvonne was to remind me later, Speer did indeed use this design for one of his proposed monumental buildings for Adolph Hitler. Anyway, it was impressive and quite modern looking. All for a queen pharaoh, you say. Yes, and what a queen pharaoh. Hatshepsut was the daughter of King Thutmose I. She became queen when she married her half-brother Thutmose II who later died young. Hatshepsut had a stepson, Thutmose III and acted as his regent while he was growing up. Later, due to a power vacuum of some sort, she took on full powers as a pharaoh, sometimes sporting a fake beard to conceal the fact that she was a woman pharaoh.

However, she was a productive pharaoh. She undertook ambitious building projects around Thebes (Luxor) including the temple of Deir el-Bahri. She also expanded Egyptian trade and brought back untold riches of ivory, ebony and gold from sub-Saharan Africa.

Following her rule, her stepson Thutmose III went on to rule for thirty more years but he tried to erase all evidence of Hatshepsut's rule to ensure that his dynasty's line of male succession was secure. All evidence of her rule was indeed erased except of course for Dier-el-Bahri. In 2007 Hatshepsut's mummy was discovered and is now housed in the Egyptian Museum in Cairo.

So with this bit of background, we can now proceed. While the temple did look impressive from a distance, as we got closer, it lost some of its mystery to me. It simply was a massive portico with no real inner chamber. It became a collection of blocks, pillars and faded inscriptions. However, it was cool inside the portico and we lingered concentrating on what pictorial representations and inscriptions there were.

**Pharaoh Queen Hatshepsut**

**Interior Deir el-Bahri**

As we were turning to go, we were met with a hoard of young Egyptian kids on a school field trip. With all their noise and screwing around, they struck me like kids anywhere. But then I realized this group was quite fortunate. I mean, how many student field trips take in one of the most significant monuments of ancient Egypt? Such a field trip was probably rare for Egyptian school kids in general unless you lived nearby such as these kids most likely did.

The reality is in their day to day lives, most Egyptians hardly ever think about the glories of the ancients. Most probably never see all these monuments. Almost all the tourists we encountered here were foreigners.

*Africa: Around the Edges*

**Field Trip**

Back on the bus, we drove over to the Colossi of Memnon and glanced at the two 64-foot high statues of the Pharaoh Amenhotep III (1351 BC). Their function was to guard the gates of the valley tomb sites. Our stay was brief, just long enough to snap a few photos.

**Colossi of Memnon**

Following that, we drove over to the Valley of the Queens for a look at where the queens and the royal princesses of Egypt were entombed including the queen of Ramses II, Nefertari.

**Valley of the Queens**

To me, it looked like a mini Valley of the Kings and the catch was you had to pay extra to go through it to see the Nefertari tomb, some 1200 LE or about seventy dollars. Another last-minute tomb rip-off. It didn't matter to me anyway because I was tired of tramping around looking at tombs so I stayed on the bus in air-conditioned comfort and read. Yvonne went out momentarily and then decided that she too had had enough tomb gazing and came back on the bus. Those that did ante up the 70-dollars came back raving about Nefertari's tomb and how well preserved it was with its colorful reliefs. Well, good for them.

And that was it for tomb viewing for the day. Now it was time for a late lunch. Doaa had mentioned that we were in for a treat. We were going to have lunch with a real farm family that she had encountered on an earlier trip. "This will be your chance to see how real Egyptians live. The Ahmeds are not poor by Egyptian standards. They are fairly prosperous but live modestly and their prepared food is superb."

O.K. Looking forward to it.

We bussed it back to the Nile and drove along the river road for a while until we pulled up in front of a modest but modern looking house situated in the midst of farmland. We piled out of the bus and walked over to a shaded outdoor patio area full of picnic tables and chairs all set

*Africa: Around the Edges*

with lunch ware, obviously waiting for us. So we sat our weary asses down and let the show begin.

**Ahmed's Lunch**

Within minutes, the feed was underway, with one course following another with various assortments of cooked vegetables, several kinds of rice and the main entrée was a delicious barbequed chicken. This along with sweet drinks, Coca-Cola and of course bottled water. No beer or wine here. The Ahmeds were, after all, observant Muslims but they were a nice family. The father spoke excellent English. His eldest son also spoke English and gave a little recitation about their farm life and his goals in education. He wanted to study to be an engineer so he could help Egypt build its infrastructure projects such as canals, dams and highways.

Following lunch, Mr. Ahmed demonstrated his reed-weaving prowess which resulted in the construction of some very sturdy furniture.

**Reed Weaving**

We then went out back to see his barnyard with its chickens and cows. After that, we went out front to examine his farm fields on the shores of the Nile.

**Ahmed's Farm**

All in all, a very pleasant and interesting glimpse into Egyptian farm life. As Doaa often put it, "The typical Egyptian farm family will never starve. They always grow enough food to eat and sell as surplus. All they need is a plot of land, a cow, some chickens and they are self-sufficient." The Ahmeds certainly showed us that.

\*\*\*

After our interlude with the Ahmeds, we boarded the bus and made our way back to Luxor and our new hotel digs, the Steigenberger Luxor Palace Nile hotel where we were to stay for a night before flying back to Cairo.

**Luxor Palace Nile Hotel**

We checked in and relaxed for an hour or so and then I went out and wandered around this elegant, somewhat old-fashioned resort hotel on the Nile. You could almost imagine Agatha Christie staying here with an assortment of her fictional characters.

That night dinner was on our own. Yvonne snacked on an orange and some bread and cheese that she had confiscated at breakfast. I went down to the bar and had a couple of Stella beers along with potato chips, peanuts, sliced carrots and celery. That was my dinner. Quite sufficient after a hearty lunch.

There was supposed to be a troupe of authentic Egyptian dancers performing in the open-air lobby at seven but when they came on, they looked like hotel employees dressed up and danced accordingly. I just went back upstairs and watched CNN International.

Oh, I should mention that the internet connection was great at this hotel so I sent my daughter Vanessa and son Colin a couple of emails informing them that all was well and no, we hadn't been captured by terrorists. Up to now the internet for the tour group had been spotty or none at all, especially around Aswan which was a declared military zone. So no private Wi-Fi or internet connection was permitted at all for civilians.

So that was it for Luxor with all its ancient monuments now swirling into a confusing blend in my addled brains. Good thing I took some notes to keep this all straight. Tomorrow Cairo.

# 11. CAIRO

**Tue. March 12**

Not much to say here, thank God. Our flight back to Cairo was at 1:30 p.m. Doaa had encouraged us to go out on our own in the morning and look around the town of Luxor, maybe revisit the market. Yvonne and I ignored her advice and decided to lounge around the hotel. The only outing I did was to an ATM bank machine across the street to get some Egyptian pounds. Even though a single Egyptian pound was worth only about 17 US cents and they went fast when tipping the one-dollar equivalent. I took out a thousand ELs, then later realized that it was only about sixty bucks. I knew that that would not last long.

Around noon we boarded our tour bus and made our way out to the airport for the Egyptian Air flight. This was about a one hour flight but they did serve a quickie lunch that was delicious with spiced BBQ lamb with rice. That along with a Stella beer did the trick. Before we knew it we had landed at the Cairo International Airport and then had to endure an hour ride through traffic back to the Kempinski hotel arriving late afternoon.

Once settled, Yvonne and I went up on the roof for a swim in their heated pool, admired the Nile again and then watched the late afternoon sun sink low over the urban horizon. Except for a modest "on-our-own" dinner which we had delivered to our room that was it for the day.

**Wed. March 13**

This was our first full day of sightseeing in Cairo beginning with a drive through the oldest section of the city. This was a labyrinthine section full of markets, souks, narrow alleyways, merchant stalls and a high wall behind which was located the oldest Coptic Church in Cairo often called the Church of the Caverns. But it is also known as the Church of the Martyrs: Sts. Sergius and Bacchus. Those two were Roman soldiers who were martyred for their Christian faith in 296 AD.

Doaa told us that the 11th-century church was built over a cave where supposedly Joseph, Mary and baby Jesus took shelter after fleeing to Egypt to escape persecution from King Herod of Judea. All of this we saw depicted on various icons lining the church walls. Doaa later led us to a library of sorts in the church which had several ancient Coptic manuscripts on display all in what looked like Arabic but may have been Coptic Egyptian.

After looking around for a while in the main nave and noting the 4th-century pillars and the brick structure interlaced with blinding white mortar, we descended some stairs to the cave which was a crypt honoring the holy family.

**Church of the Caverns**

*Africa: Around the Edges*

Icons

Coptic Manuscript

**Holy Family Cave**

O.K. all duly noted. Kind of creepy. Now let me out of here and into fresh air.

Right outside we were greeted by a pleasant old woman, whom Doaa explained was a Coptic and who posed for pictures for a small price. I couldn't resist since she looked like she had come from the 11th century itself.

**Coptic Worshipper**

All of this made me wonder what the Coptic Church was all about. I think my first encounter with the notion of Coptics in Egypt came from reading Lawrence Durrell's "Justine," the first book in his Alexandria Quartet. One of the main characters was Nessim, the cuckolded husband of Justine. Nessim was a wealthy Coptic banker engaged in some mysterious gun-running operation for the Jews while they fought the Arabs and the British in order to establish the state of Israel.

In "Justine," Durrell has his character Nessim claim that the Coptics had been the brains of the Egyptian Empire and had run it from the days when Christianity was established in the first century, right through the time when the Arabs took over in the 7th century and established the Islamic religion. Even so, Nessim claimed it was still the Coptics who were operating at the highest levels of the Islamic government and kept everything going.

Coptic followers further claim that the Coptic Christian religion is the original and purest form of Christianity that was established when St. Mark came to Egypt in 42 AD proselytizing about the newly formed religion.

Still, many elements of the Coptic religion appear to be borrowed directly from the ancient Egyptian religions that evolved into their concept of the Holy Trinity. This is backed up by several modern-day Egyptian historians including Jason Thompson who in his book "A History of Egypt," noted that the Egyptian gods--Osiris, Isis and Horus are often taken as an allegory of the Holy Family. Isis easily equated to Mary, Horus to Jesus, and of course Osiris to God himself.

It was their concept of what they believed to be the true nature of Christ that led the Coptics to breakaway in the 5th century from the dominant school of Christian thought, namely that Christ was a mix of being fully human and fully divine. Coptics believed that Christ had two separate natures, one human and one divine but without intermingling. Despite that Coptics were accused of believing that Christ had only one nature, a divine nature. Forget the human side. Talk about splitting hairs! My head is still spinning over that one.

Of course today, the Coptics comprise only about fifteen percent of the Egyptian population and have been subject to a series of terrorist attacks on their churches by Islamic extremists. Egyptian President El-Sisi has declared war on those who attack the Coptics because as far as he is concerned, he wants Egypt to remain a secular state, even though he is a Muslim himself. I saw this declaration myself on a plaque outside the church.

**El-Sisi Support**

Our first full day in Egypt, Yvonne and I had observed an elaborate Coptic wedding reception at the Kempinski Hotel. Everybody looked prosperous and very western in their sharply tailored clothes. The women were quite beautiful in that Egyptian way and certainly not restrained by any religious prohibitions.

Following the Church of the Caverns, we walked over to yet another Coptic Church, the so-called "Hanging Church" from the $7^{th}$ century. Perched upon the ruins of an old Roman fortress, this church was once the headquarters for the Coptic Church in Egypt. We didn't spend much time here but were informed that it was known as the site of several visions of Mary. We did spot an icon of the patron saint of the Coptic religion, St. Mark himself.

*Africa: Around the Edges*

**St. Mark**

Now being done with the Coptic churches, we took a quick look at a nearby Jewish synagogue that was defunct. Doaa told us that few Jews were left in Egypt. Many had fled when Gamal Nasser came to power in 1956.

Next, we bussed it over to the Citadel of Saladin that dominated the city skyline. Built high on a hill overlooking Cairo, the citadel was built by the Arab conqueror, Saladin around 1176 to ward off Christian crusaders. The citadel included three mosques, one of which was the Mosque of Muhammad Ali, ruler of Egypt in the 1830s and 1840s and also known as the father of modern Egypt. We didn't have much time here except to dash in and take a quick look around at the cavernous interior. Then later, I took a couple of shots of a head-scarfed tourist outside along with a view of highly polluted Cairo.

**Mosque Interior**

**Respectful Tourist**

**Polluted Cairo**

Pant, pant, pant. We were running out of energy doing all this church and mosque hopping. Finally, it was one o'clock and time for lunch so we repaired to a nearby park which featured a nice restaurant in the midst of spectacular landscaping with fountains and statuary. Here we dined on yet more BBQ chicken, well done with all the expectant side dishes. I tried to order a Stella beer with this but Yvonne warned me that I would be in no shape to concentrate on the wonders of the Cairo Museum scheduled for later this afternoon. So I opted for a large ice tea. However, probably having overeaten, I still felt rather sluggish and sleepy. However, skipping the Cairo Museum was unthinkable because the Cairo Museum was one of those must "sees" in Egypt.

**Dining in the Park**

**Cairo Museum**

From the outside, despite being an elegant looking building, the Cairo Museum was by no means on the scale of what I had expected. I was used to the Field Museum or the Museum of Science and Industry which covered many acres on the Chicago lakefront. But no matter because within this museum was housed the most significant treasures of ancient Egypt.

I should also note that out in Giza, a mega-museum is almost complete that will house all the holdings of the Cairo Museum plus thousands of other ancient Egyptian artifacts. The idea is to have a grouping of major tourist attractions in the same area as the pyramids. Below is an artist's conception of what the Grand Egyptian Museum will look like. The new museum is scheduled to open sometime in 2020.

**Grand Egyptian Museum**

O.K., so now we can take a look at the highlights of what I saw in the old Cairo Museum. First up was a spectacular hallway of giant Egyptian statuary of various ancient periods. However much of the hallway was undergoing renovations and some of the statues were under wraps.

**Main Hallway**

As usual, Doaa led the group off to lecture them on particular artifacts that she thought important and I stayed behind. I hate being guided through a museum. I would rather explore on my own and focus on those items that capture my interest. And of course, snap a picture of them.

In the Old Kingdom section on the ground floor, I stopped and pondered an assemblage of an ancient Egyptian river vessel. This appeared to be a recent acquisition since it was still being worked on.

**Ancient Nile River Boat**

Also, on the same floor, I ran into a well-preserved statue of what appeared to be a seated scribe taking dictation.

**Scribe**

Moving on, I paused before some very lifelike granite Sphinxes from 1800 BC. My guide book referred to these as looking like the cowardly lion from the Wizard of Oz. Not quite.

**Granite Sphinx**

Buzzing through the rest of the ground level floor probably missing much that was important or rather seeing these items but not photographing them, I went upstairs to the second level to check out the Tutankhamun Galleries, one of the most significant holdings of the museum.

*Africa: Around the Edges*

**Tut Chamber Layout**

After looking at some of the artifacts found in his tomb, I entered the hallowed chamber of King Tut himself. There under glass was his golden mask. Or was it? I was confused. I had seen the exact same thing in his tomb in the Valley of the Kings. Which one was real? It is claimed that his mummified body was indeed in his renovated tomb in the Valley of the Kings. However, seeing his golden mask here in the Cairo Museum, it was never clear to me what was real and what was not.

**King Tut Golden Mask**

Anyway, even though it was forbidden, I snapped a photo of the golden mask and right away, a guard accosted me saying it was forbidden as he reached for my camera. I yanked it away and retreated from the chamber with him following me and demanding that I delete the photo. I said maybe, but as I took off, I told myself fat chance.

Once out of the chamber and into the next room I slowed down and took a photo of King Tut's ornate, gold-encrusted throne.

**Tut's Golden Throne**

**Mummy Room**

Next up was the mummy room as seen in this stock photo. This room, arguably the most famous room in the museum, featured mummies of the most famous pharaohs including Ramses II. Of course, in order to see this, you had to pay extra and of course, photography was forbidden. This time I put away my camera because the security guard in this room was a big hulking dude armed with a pistol.

When I came to the unwrapped mummy of Ramses II, I was struck by how small he was. According to the mummy experts probably around five-six, somewhat small by Egyptian great warrior standards. Also, as shown in this stock photo, he had a very peaky nose possibly indicating he was far from handsome. Then there was his outstretched hand indicating that it had once held a royal scepter of sorts called an Ankh symbol.

**Mummy of Ramses II**

Actually, for being 90-years old when he died, Ramses II looked to be in fairly good shape. Overall, though the mummy room was somewhat spooky. You almost felt like a few of these guys could come alive at any moment. Then again, maybe I had seen too many "Curse of the Mummy" movies.

To lighten the mood somewhat, I headed over to the next room that housed the mummified animals. First up was a mummified dog. Did Egyptians have dogs as pets? I later learned that they did indeed along with cats, monkeys and falcons. Also that they kept lions, elephants and hippos.

*Africa: Around the Edges*

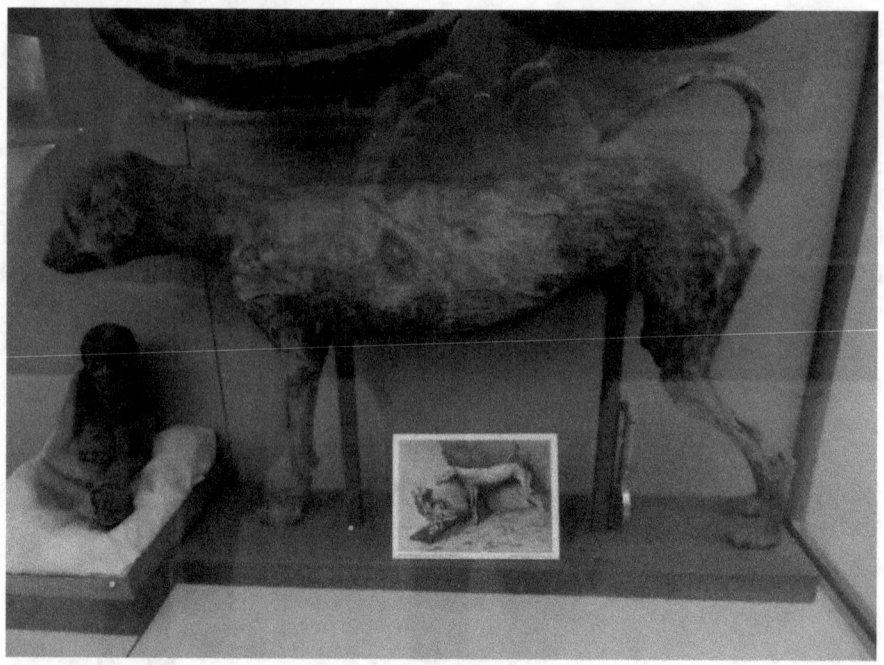

**Mummified Dog**

Still, one of the main attractions in this section were the mummified cats, large cats, small cats. I had heard that some of these cats were raised to be sacrificed and mummified because of their special powers in Egyptian mythology in which they would have an afterlife along with the pharaoh. Maybe. I don't know how the cats felt about this but probably not good. In any case, aren't cats supposed to have nine lives?

**Mummified Cat**

After the animal mummies, I returned to the main entrance, sat down and waited for the others to return which they did a few minutes later. A few remarking that there was too much to absorb in the relatively short time that we had spent here, about an hour and a half. This despite Doaa's expert guidance. I didn't care. I had my photos, legal and illegal, and that's all that counted for me.

It was now past four and we were done for the day. We bussed it back to the Hotel Kempinski where Yvonne and I chilled and ordered dinner through room service. Tomorrow was the last day of our tour with Odyssey and we would be visiting the most ancient of all the pyramids, the step pyramid of Saqqara as well as ruins of the ancient Egyptian capital Memphis.

# 12. MEMPHIS/ SAQQARA

**Thur. March 14**

So here it was. Our last day with Odyssey. And it was on this day that we were going to see probably the most important pyramid of the entire Egyptian civilization. That of Saqqara, a step pyramid that predated all other classic pyramids by at least a hundred years. However, first, we were going to see an even more ancient site, namely the ruins of Memphis. Memphis was once the capital of Egypt founded by King Menes, (c. 3150 BC) who united the two lands of Egypt into a single country. It remained the capital of the Old Kingdom until around 2181 BC.

At 10 a.m. sharp, we boarded our tour bus and made our way, through heavy traffic to the outskirts of Cairo. Then by-passing the pyramids of Giza, we kept on going into the countryside for another twenty kilometers. At first appearance, this was cultivated countryside with palm trees lining the road. Indeed, this was the first time I had seen so many palm trees together in Egypt, resembling a palm tree orchard.

**Palm Orchard**

By and by, we arrived at the Memphis site. At first, there wasn't much to see. No ruins of any sort were initially apparent, only a bunch of tourist stands and a merchant tossing food to a large gathering of dogs.

**Dog Gathering**

Eventually, we spotted the first major attraction of Memphis, namely another sphinx. But this one was unique in that it was carved out of alabaster. It was rather large and impressive representing some pharaoh but nobody was quite sure which one.

**Alabaster Sphinx**

Following that, we walked over to a pavilion that housed the Colossus of Ramses II. As we entered and walked around on an elevated rampway staring at this monster, we had to admit that at 69-feet tall and weighing some eighty tons, it was impressive.

**Colossus of Ramses II**

Of course, this statue had been installed in Memphis during the days of Ramses II's reign well after Memphis was no longer the Egyptian capital. That was the deal back in the time of Ramses II and other pharaohs. Egyptian pharaohs would not only build their own new monuments, but they would also pepper the more ancient monuments with their statues and reliefs and inscriptions, just so they were everywhere and so that nobody would forget them. This is especially the case with Ramses II who as we noted earlier, had a real PR sense.

After our look around Memphis, we headed over to the site of the Saqqara Pyramid which we could see hovering tantalizing in the distance. But before we got there, Doaa wanted us to stop and see several important tombs near the Saqqara complex. So I dutifully followed Doaa around with the others.

First, we came to the tombs of King Teti of the Old Kingdom (c. 2350 BC). One of the tombs was that of Teti's daughter, Idut. Inside we saw depicted the everyday life of the Egyptians as well as an image of a hippo giving birth and a crocodile right behind him ready to ready to eat the baby and then an image of the princesses herself.

**Crocodile Attacking Hippo**

**Princess Idut**

After viewing a couple of more tombs, we finally hiked over to the official entrance to the Saqqara pyramid which was impressive itself. Billed as the Funerary of Djoser, the pharaoh at the time, it was a walled-in compound that once surrounded the whole Saqqara complex. We entered it through a narrow passageway and then made our way along a colonnade until we came out onto the grounds of the step pyramid itself, Saqqara.

**Funerary of Djoser**

**Colonnade**

This pyramid was an impressive sight, indeed. Designed by the famous ancient Egyptian architect, Imhotep, around 2667 BC, Saqqara is the earliest example of formal pyramid building in Egypt. Built up in platform steps, it had a stability that ensured it stood for centuries. Often later pyramids with the classic steep rising peaks would collapse or crumble away. Of course, they looked a lot sleeker initially, especially when covered in white limestone. However, it was here at Saqqara where it all began.

**Saqqara Step Pyramid**

In the end, we didn't spend much time here. All we could do is stop and gaze at the pyramid and take photos. One could go inside if one wished, but Doaa said there wasn't much to see, no inscriptions or images. After fifteen minutes or so of staring at this iconic pyramid, we headed back out of the grounds.

I was getting hungry but we were not done yet with the Saqqara complex. Doaa led us over to the Imhotep Museum which opened a few years ago and which housed many masterpieces found in the tombs including small statues, vessels, engraved stele and ancient tools used to build the monuments.

What I liked best were a couple of steles engraved with a heraldic and demotic script from four thousand years ago. It was as if ghosts were speaking to us through the millenniums.

**Saqqara Stele**

After twenty minutes or so of wandering around this fascinating museum, we finally boarded the bus and headed over towards a countryside restaurant for a late lunch. But wait, not quite yet. For some reason, we had to stop again and check out a workshop school where Egyptian kids and older people learned traditional Egyptian handicrafts. All very impressive, especially the baking of the bread which we sampled and made our stomachs growl even more for lunch.

**Baking Bread**

Soon we were back on the bus and heading towards the restaurant recommended by Doaa. It was indeed a countryside eatery with palm trees galore but it was also a vast tourist dining complex with yards of tables and benches under a canvas.

At that point, we didn't care. We all sat down and ordered mucho Stella beer. Then seconds later, the food arrived, huge quantities of it, lamb, chicken, beef with all the sides. Doaa warned us not to eat too much since we were going to have a big farewell feed later that evening. Nonetheless, we chowed down like starving Armenians (bad taste joke, sorry) and of course, gulped down vast quantities of Stella beer.

A half-hour later, stuffed, half drunk and wobbly, we returned to our bus and headed back into the traffic mayhem that was Cairo. However, as we approached the center city, a cop car that had been escorting us from the restaurant, started flashing his lights and blowing his siren. He then took the lead, sirens wailing and lights flashing and we cut through the dense traffic like a knife through butter with everyone pulling off to the side. Now that was the way to deal with Cairo traffic and at the same time ensure your security. It was a fitting end to all our going about in Cairo and its environs.

When we returned to the hotel, both Yvonne and I were stuffed and pooped out from all the sightseeing. I lounged on the rooftop, Stella in hand while Yvonne took to the bed.

**Tired Yvonne**

That evening, we had a cocktail hour in the top floor bar of the hotel with the big views of Cairo with all its lights ablaze. In addition to the socializing and congratulating ourselves on holding up throughout this marathon tour of Egypt, we had a final exam of sorts. Doaa had insisted that we assume the identity of a particular ancient Egyptian or a god and talk about their life and accomplishments. When Doaa first mentioned this a couple of days ago, some in our group were resistant making comments like, "I didn't sign on to be a student again." "No homework please, I'm too old." But in the end, all relented and here is how it went.

Yvonne, one of the first up, pretended to be Sobek, the crocodile god of the waters and war. She went on at length about this god Sobek that was associated with pharaonic power, fertility, and military prowess and protector of the dangers of the Nile. Others pretended to be Ramses II, Nefertari, Imhotep, most giving rather charming accounts. Except for Mick, who just talked about his days of escorting Egyptian President Anwar Sadat around in 1978 in Washington DC with Israel Prime Menachem Begin. That was when the Sadat and Begin signed a historic peace agreement between Egypt and Israel at President Carter's Camp David retreat.

I took a different tack. I assumed the identity of Menenhetet, the main fictional character in Norman Mailer's mega-novel, "Ancient Evenings." I explained that through reincarnation and the ability to read minds, Menenhetet witnessed a hundred and sixty years of critical times for the Egyptian empire starting with the reign of Ramses II and up to and during the reign of Ramses IX (1129 BC).

At first, Menenhetet was the chief warrior in Ramses II's army during the battle of Kadesh. Then because Ramses' pet lion was killed during the battle and because Menenhetet was in charge of the beast, he was exiled to oversee the mines of northern Nubia. Later back in good graces of Ramses, he was put in charge of Ramses' harem. It was here he met his first demise while seducing Ramses' wife, Nefertari. Ramses eldest warrior son caught him in the act and stabbed him in the back.

Next, a reborn Menenhetet began the quiet life of a scribe and a priest eventually becoming trusted Visier to the Pharaoh. But soon bored with that, Menenhetet decided to build up his riches by allying himself with the tomb robbers of the Valley of the Kings. The re-incarnation processes repeat several times because Menenhetet usually died early until the time of Ramses IX when he dies for real and the story ends.

I also briefly described all the incestuous goings-on in the royal court between brothers and sisters, mothers and sons, fathers and daughters, and whatever else you can imagine. Most people got a kick out of that.

After our cocktail hour, we repaired to the restaurant downstairs and feasted on yet another great meal and then said our goodbyes to our fellow group members and to Doaa herself.

When I mentioned that we were traveling to Alexandria for four days, Doaa replied, "Oh, I live in Alexandria. Why don't you contact me, and I will prepare you a great meal. Then if you want I can take you around and show you Alexandria."

I thought about it for a second and then observed that she was probably tired of touring with tourists and needed a rest. She protested, saying not at all. "At least come for a meal."

Yvonne chimed in at this point said, "That would be lovely. We have your phone number. We'll be in contact."

It turned out that we never did contact Doaa. We wanted our time in Alexandria to be strictly for ourselves so we could chill and not run around helter-skelter. That was the last we were to see of Doaa, an excellent guide but also an agent of overload on Egyptian lore.

Following dinner, we returned to our room and turned in. And that was it, the end of our Odyssey tour. From here on, we were on our own in the crazy and sometimes dangerous land of Egypt.

# 13. ALEXANDRIA

**Fri. March 15**

Yvonne and I were sound asleep when the Odyssey Tour group departed at the ungodly hour of 4 a.m. About half were going home, the rest flying on to Jordan for a four-day tour of Jordan including Petra, the ancient stone city carved into cliffs. Now we wanted to see Petra too but found it odd that it would be included in a tour to Egypt rather than one to Israel and Jordan, a tour that we might someday take.

However, as I explained before, as long as we were going to Egypt, I couldn't resist a visit to Alexandria what with all its ancient Greek and Roman history and of course, its immortalization in Lawrence Durrell's "Alexandria Quartet." As far as I was concerned, it was a must-see even though a lot of its ancient past was still buried under the modern city and/ or wiped out by urban renewal. It was still Alexandria and it still had the most spectacular setting of all the Egyptian cities sitting as it did on the Mediterranean coast. Also, we wanted to visit nearby Alamein, the site of one of the most important North African battles during World War II.

So it was, we said goodbye to Hotel Kempinski and at 8 a.m. we boarded a minivan on a pre-arranged ride to Alexandria. Perhaps word here about this pre-arranged ride. Initially, I checked out going to Alexandria by train. That was certainly do-able and cheap. Still, Yvonne wasn't sure about that for security reasons. After all, we would be on our own in a very turbulent society without the protections of a tour group. To calm her, I booked a private driving trip to Alexandria through the hotel.

The catch was that it was rather expensive since I had to pay for a car rental and the services of not only a driver but also for an English speaking tour guide who was coming along too. I had no choice in the matter. At 400-dollars this smelled like a rip-off but I went ahead anyway and booked the deal. I figured at least we would get a half-day guided tour of Alexandria as well as someone to point out the sights along the way through northern Egypt.

This all worked out rather well. I made some interesting discoveries on the far northern outskirts of Cairo as we drove along the major expressway to Alexandria. Here we saw one outstanding apartment and housing development after another. Our guide, Omar, told us that these were homes for the poor as well as the middle class. It was all part of a new town development project to disperse the overcrowded population of Cairo. All the apartments and homes appeared quite modern, clean and tidy. It reminded me of the home building one sees on the outskirts of Las Vegas.

**New Homes**

Farther along, we drove by a lot of industrial enterprises recently built and a couple of expensive looking shopping malls with signs touting their brand name merchandise. About halfway through our 218 kilometer journey to Alexandria, we stopped at a cafe at one such mall in Sadat City and partook of a few sweet cakes and cups of coffee.

**Industry**

**Mall Cafe**

North of these developments we drove through an agricultural area that produced palm dates, figs, avocados, and other fruits thanks to new irrigation systems that had been installed. All part of El-Sisi's efforts to modernize Egyptian agriculture.

Later we passed by what remained of the delta marshland that once surrounded Alexandria, giving us a sense of a more rural Egypt.

**Delta Marshland**

Around 11:30, we entered the outskirts of Alexandria but because the main boulevard to the waterfront was shut down for street repairs, we had to wind our way through the narrow side streets to get there. As we made our way through these streets, Alexandria didn't look much different from Cairo. Junky and trashy with crammed together buildings. At the street level, we passed various shops and vendors with men lounging outside on chairs smoking their hookahs. Others observed the noon call to prayer by kneeling on their small portable prayer rugs.

**Back Streets**

After a tedious half-hour of this, we finally, we came out to the waterfront boulevard and there was Alexandria in all its postcard glory.

**Alexandria**

We drove past our hotel, Hotel Cecil, but did not stop there because our tour guide was eager to show us some of the highlights of Alexandria's ancient past. Even though we were yearning to check-in, we yielded to his demand in part because I wanted to get my money's worth out of this day.

***

First up was the open-air museum, the ancient Serapeum on a hill overlooking the city. Founded around 222 BC by Ptolemy III, this patch of land contained hundreds of artifacts right up through the Hellenistic and Roman period until the early Christians took over. It's most intriguing features were a series of underground catacombs and Pompey's Pillar situated up higher on the hillside. Before we got to that Omar showed us around pointing out the various statues, busts and sarcophagi from the time of Alexander the Great who founded the city around 332 BC.

**Serapeum**

Once done with that, we entered a temple reconstruct that led to the catacombs which honeycombed the ground around here. This was by far the spookiest underground experience of our whole time in Egypt.

First, there were several levels to the catacombs each with its own series of enclaves. Now I have seen the catacombs in Rome for Christian burials but these were far more intriguing. These catacombs housed scores of sarcophagi of important ancient Alexandrians and statues of various Greco-Roman and Egyptian gods such as the Egyptian god Anubis who was depicted with the head of a jackal. As a result, a lot of jackals were sacrificed here. Call the Animal cruelty society. Of course, all this mishmash of religion was encouraged by Ptolemy rulers who wanted everybody to be happy no matter what religion they followed.

**Serapeum Catacombs**

Everything ended for Serapeum when the Roman Emperor Constantine came to power in 4th century AD and converted to Christianity. He then set about persecuting all the pagans in the Roman Empire. In particular, in 389 AD, a Christian mob led by Pope Theophilus of Alexandria rampaged through and destroyed the Serapeum. After wandering around in this underground maze for a half hour or so, we emerged and hiked over to Pompey's Pillar.

**Pompey's Pillar**

This was a 21-meter high column done in the Roman Corinthian Style. It was constructed in 297 AD commemorating the victory of Roman Emperor Diocletian over the Alexandrian revolt. Actually, the tower had nothing to do with the Pompey who ruled Alexandria in 48 BC. Still, the pillar was impressive as we wandered around it but compared to the ancient Egyptian monuments including the obelisks that we had seen, it ran a poor second.

Following Serapeum, we drove over to the nearby ruins of a Roman amphitheater. It was pathetic looking amphitheater compared to the other Roman amphitheaters we had seen in previous trips to Arles, France, Rome, Greece and Turkey so we didn't even stop, just glanced out of the car window. This was small fare as Roman amphitheaters go, seating only seven to eight hundred people.

Omar now wanted to go straight over to one of the most spectacular sights in Alexandria, the 15th-century Citadel of Qaitbay built out on a peninsula guarding the sea approaches to Alexandria. O.K. we were game for that but when we arrived, the Citadel was mobbed by school kids.

**Citadel of Qaitbay**

We made our way through the mob up a long promenade and into the fort itself. This was a massive construct on the order of any medieval castle in Europe with similar turrets and ramparts. Built by the Sultan Al-Ashraf Qaitbay in 1477AD, it was one of the most important defensive strongholds along the Mediterranean coast up until the time of Ottoman takeover in 1517. Even then it continued to serve its defensive function under the Ottomans undergoing several renovations and one major reconstruction after the British bombed it in 1882 to put down a rebellion over British rule.

**Qaitbay Ramparts**

Reputedly, the fort was built initially from the ruins of the famous lighthouse of Alexandria, the Pharos Lighthouse that once stood on this promontory but by the late 15th century, it had perished in an earthquake.

Inside we checked out the interior of the fort with its meter-thick walls and various chambers which functioned as barracks for the soldiers and storage rooms for their weapons. This along with elaborate floors of mosaics of Islamic design.

**Mosaic Floor**

Back outside, we walked along the rampart that encircled the fort just above the crashing sea, all attesting to the defensive impregnability of this fort.

*Africa: Around the Edges*

**Fortress on the Sea**

After the citadel, Omar announced that he and the driver had to return to Cairo. Now it was only 3 p.m., so our half-day tour was only a couple of hours but at this point that was O.K. by us. We were ready to check into Hotel Cecil. They drove us over and we said goodbye, my wallet four hundred dollars lighter. Oh, well, at least we made it to Alexandria in good style.

Now our attention turned to Hotel Cecil, this legendary hotel where the rich and famous and not so rich and famous like poor writers and artists and various statesmen used to hang out. It had a rather old fashioned but pleasing facade from the street.

**Hotel Cecil**

That was what we wanted. No modernity for us in Alexandria. We were going to stick to the early 20th century and commune with the ghosts of Cecil's literary past.

As soon as we were dropped off, a bellman came outside and loaded our suitcases onto a cart. We stopped briefly at the check-in desk. All was in order and our room was awaiting. We glanced around the lobby for a few seconds and noted that the interior of the hotel was of the same early 20th century period, perhaps post World War I but obviously maintained and restored. Perfect.

Meanwhile, the bellman, Mohammed, was waiting patiently before two very ornate and ancient cage elevators which ran side by side. Mohammed loaded our suitcases in one of the cage elevators and indicated that we should take the other one.

At first, Yvonne was hesitant because she had had a close call with such an elevator in Vienna years before. Half sick, she had stepped into what she thought was the elevator cage when in fact it was the base of the elevator shaft and coming down from above was the main cage itself just feet above her head. She stepped out in time but never forgot that close call. I assured her that this elevator was much safer and appeared to be well maintained, so she reluctantly did step in as I held the elevator cage gate open.

*Africa: Around the Edges*

**Cage Elevator**

After getting settled in our spacious third-floor room in which Cecil B. DeMille had once stayed, I went out to the balcony and took a few pictures of our seafront views.

**Seafront Boulevard**

A couple of hours later, we went downstairs and I had a Stella beer in the hotel bar while perusing the Cecil dinner menu. Needless to say, it looked expensive. While we thought we might dine here at least once during our stay, we opted to go outside and look around for a cheaper restaurant.

We didn't have to look far. Right next door was such a restaurant that looked respectable. We went in and checked out the menu. Not being very hungry, we ordered a large margarita pizza and a beer.

"A beer? But monsieur, we do not serve alcohol here," came the response. "Would you care for tea or perhaps a soda drink?"

Oh, right, I thought. Still an Islamic country. No booze. I ordered a Sprite all the while wondering about the Margarita pizza. As it turned out, the pizza was well done and quite tasty.

After dining, we wandered around the small square next to the hotel, all the time being pursued by a couple of coachmen offering nighttime rides in their horse-drawn carriages along the seafront. We took a pass, saying another time and returned to our hotel room.

Day one in Alexandria over and done.

## 14. ADEL TOUR

**Sat. March 16**

First, a word here about our room. As charming and as old fashioned elegant it appeared, it had some serious shortcomings. First of all, while it had wooden shutters to cut off the noise and light from the busy seafront boulevard below, overnight cold sea breezes managed to penetrate the leaky shutters and windows and right into our room. Our covers were so scant that we were freezing. We got up in the middle of the night and draped our light ski jackets over the blankets. That worked for a while until they slid off onto the floor. When I complained to the desk later, they assured me they would leave extra blankets in our room.

Next, when I stepped into the bathtub/shower arrangement, I discovered that initially there was no hot water. However, after a few minutes, the hot water managed to make it up to the third floor but somehow it cut off the cold water entirely and the shower became scalding hot. I finagled with the single handle faucet some more and the cold water came back entirely erasing the hot water flow. That set the pattern, a few seconds of cold and then a few seconds of scalding hot. No warm water in between. Back and forth, back and forth. And that's the way I had to deal with it. I considered complaining to the front desk again but short of changing our room, nothing probably could be done. Ultimately, I decided to live with it and became quite adept at dealing with this hot/cold flow of water. At least it woke me up smartly every morning that we were there. Maybe that was what Cecil B. DeMille was smiling about in his photo portrait on the wall. But enough complaints. A tour day awaited.

***

Around 8:00 a.m., we took the cage elevator down to the first floor for our first buffet breakfast at the Cecil. When we arrived, the dining room was packed with guests and plates piled high with goodies from the buffet. We managed to find a table off in an alcove and proceeded to help ourselves to the offerings of many kinds of fruits, cereals, sausages, and of course, customized omelets. That done, we returned to our room and made ready to go out for the day.

Now I had already promised Yvonne that we would have a tour guide for our four days in Alexandria. No way did she want us to wander around on our own. However, up to now, I had made no arrangements for that, thinking that the hotel could fix us up with a knowledgeable and approved guide. So now the moment had arrived to seek out such an arrangement. I returned to the lobby and looked around for a concierge desk or an official-looking concierge type. No desk, no official concierge. Seeing me looking around, the bell captain Mohammed asked me if he could be of help.

"I'm looking for a concierge maybe to fix up a tour for us of Alexandria."

"Oh, Mr. Brown, we have no concierge as such but I can offer you my services for I am very knowledgeable about tour guides and such."

"Really?" I replied, thinking that Mohammed was presenting himself as an unofficial concierge. But then thinking he probably knew a lot about the tourist scene here.

"Yes, of course. Now, what do you require? An English speaking guide only for today or for your entire stay?"

"Uhh...depending on the guide but preferably for the rest of our stay here."

"Mr. Brown, I believe I have just the person for you. He is an Alexandrian and knows the city well. He also speaks excellent English and has a very nice taxi in which to take you around. Not only that, he is here right outside and waiting for a customer. His name is Adel."

"Sounds interesting, I said. " Why don't you introduce me?"

"Very good."

Mohammed led me outside and down a half block to a taxi stand and there sitting on a patio chair was a middle-aged man, well-groomed, well dressed. This was Adel. Upon seeing us approach, Adel rose and greeted Mohammad. Then glancing over to me with a smile, he offered his hand, apparently already knowing what this was all about.

Mohammad explained to Adel what I was interested in, namely a couple of day tours around Alexandria.

Adel nodded, "Certainly, certainly, I can offer a full-day tour that will be quite informative all for a very reasonable price of 75-dollars, US."

After yesterday's ripoff, the price did strike me as reasonable. I added that on the second day we wanted to go to El-Alamein to see the World War II battle monuments. Adel said he certainly could do that too, maybe for 100 US for the day since a lot of gas would be involved.

Embolden and still smarting from my 400-dollar voyage from Cairo to here, I asked what he would charge to drive us to the Cairo International Airport on the coming Tuesday at the end of our stay in Alexandria. He replied that would be a hundred dollars too. That price struck me as absurdly cheap, so I immediately accepted.

Adel then showed me his taxi. It was a late model Toyota sedan, very spacious and clean. Even verging on luxurious. It was certainly good enough to haul us around Alexandria and to the Cairo airport.

So the deal was set. I called up to Yvonne to get moving because we indeed had an English speaking tour guide. When she came down all ready to go sightseeing, she greeted Adel, chatted a minute and then told me later that he appeared to be a fine gentleman and in some ways reminded her late father, Fred.

**Adel & Yvonne**

Meanwhile, Mohammed was beaming at this arrangement which appeared to be a success. I thought that maybe he would be getting a cut of this. Who knew? Anyway, a few minutes later we were off for a day of sightseeing with Adel.

As we pulled out into traffic, I was struck again by how crazy Alexandrian drivers were. It was all about playing chicken with other cars. Adel was an expert at this, nosing his vehicle into oncoming traffic, missing other vehicles that never slowed down or a few who stopped only inches away from contact. Then Adel finding tight drive-through spaces in a traffic-jammed street where most vehicles were stalled, spaces that I could never discern. However, the going was a lot better when we got out onto the major boulevards and were soon driving through nicer neighborhoods flanked by mansions, embassies, private colleges and schools.

Soon we arrived at our first stop of the day, the Alexandria National Museum. The museum was housed in an Italian Style Palace which was once home to the U.S. consulate according to Adel.

**Alexandria National Museum**

Inside, we found a sampling from each period of Egyptian history--Ancient, the Hellenic, the Roman, the Coptic and of course, the Islamic. In other words, this little museum covered a lot of ground. However, for some reason, the collection that struck us as the most spectacular were the panels of Coptic icons. I don't know. Maybe we were tired of the ancient and in a more religious mode.

**Coptic Icons**

In any case, we only spent an hour here because we still had a lot of sightseeing ahead. We returned to Adel who had been waiting patiently outside by his taxi. We then drove off to see the newly built Alexandria Library, officially called the Bibliotheca Alexandrina.

**Bibliotheca Alexandrina**

As we approached the entrance, we were impressed with the massive curved granite wall engraved with ancient Egyptian inscriptions. From an aerial view photograph that we saw later, the library appeared to be a tipsy flying saucer plunging into the Mediterranean. Modern architecture, I guess.

**Aerial View**

However, once inside, the design of the library made dazzling sense. We signed up for a tour and listened to the guide on how this library came to be.

The history lesson went like this: The ancient library of Alexandria, extolled around the known world at the time, was the penultimate repository of ancient knowledge. Founded by the Athenian scholar Demetrius of Phaleron during the reign of King Ptolemy II around 285 BC, the library was part of the larger institution of higher learning known as the Alexandria "Mouseion" dedicated to the Muses.

The holdings of more than 40-thousand manuscripts were divided by subject: rhetoric, law, history, medicine, mathematics, natural science and humanities. All were written on papyrus in Greek and in the now extinct Egyptian language. Scholars from around the ancient world came here to study this vast array of ancient knowledge.

Now as to its destruction. Being located near the harbor at the time, the library was vulnerable to naval shore battles. Thus, it happened that the greater part of the ancient library was destroyed in 48 BC when Julius Caesar intervened in a civil war between Cleopatra and Ptolemy XIII. At one point, Caesar set the harbor ships on fire to clear the harbor. Apparently, sparks from the flaming ships drifted over and set the library on fire. An accident or on purpose? Who knows?

A second branch of the library located inside a temple dedicated to Serapis, a Ptolemy god, was destroyed in 391 AD when the Christian Roman Emperor Theodosius ordered all pagan temples to be destroyed. That effectively finished off all traces of the ancient library except it lived on in legend and myth throughout the centuries until today.

As our guide explained, the whole point of this modern library extravaganza was to establish Alexandria as a city of world-renowned learning once again. Just looking at its interior, we could see that it might be achieving its goal with its vast multi-level subject holdings and endless research desks all wired up with the latest digital technology.

**Main Reading Room**

However, perusing the stacks later, we discovered it wasn't all state-of-the-art. Yvonne, a former art librarian, noted that they still followed the Dewey system in its shelf organization. Of course, she paused and checked out the art history holdings and deemed them to be sufficient. We also saw collections of ancient texts, most likely of the Koran.

**Ancient Text**

One could spend days here browsing around or just staring out the expansive windows at the ever-present Mediterranean. But of course, we had to move on.

Next up was a return to the 20th century and a look at Egyptian King Farouk's jewelry mansion a few blocks away. We were going there at the insistence of Adel who claimed it was a must-see in Alexandria. O.K. Now who was King Farouk you might ask? Farouk was the last ruler of the Muhammad Ali dynasty. You may remember the ruler Muhammad Ali from my earlier reference to him as being the father of modern Egypt in the 19th century.

Farouk was born in 1920 and died in 1965 at age 45 basically from overeating. He was once described as a "stomach with a head." He was also a playboy with many mistresses and forced to abdicate his throne in 1952 after which he went into exile. I remembered Farouk from newsreels in my youth during the fifties. Boy, he was gross.

*Africa: Around the Edges*

**King Farouk**

Nonetheless, Farouk had inherited an amazing collection of jewelry amassed during the reign of the Muhammad Ali dynasty which spanned almost 150 years. Some of the most spectacular items of this collection were now on display in this mansion which once belonged to his sister, Princess Fatimas.

First, we took a look at the mansion itself. Certainly imposing but not large as far as mansions go but very luxurious once we went inside.

**Royal Jewelry Museum**

Needless to say, the place was crammed with overflowing displays of jewelry. Here are some of the items that caught our eye.

**Amethyst Necklace**

*Africa: Around the Edges*

**Makeup Compacts**

**Writing Set**

After a half-hour of nosing around here and watching Yvonne examine the holdings with a jeweler's eye, we moved on.

Next up, Adel wanted to show us Farouk's beachfront mansion on the edge of town. On the way, Yvonne and I once again marveled at the seafront boulevard which appeared to go on forever. It did have a formal name: El-Gaish Road but most Alexandrians referred to it as "The Corniche." Whatever you called it, it was spectacular as it ran by a series of luxury hotels and mansions on the land side and on the seaside, offered great views of the Mediterranean. This boulevard easily ranks right up there with the oceanfront boulevard of Cannes.

**Mamoura Royal Gardens**

Soon we came to Mamoura Royal Gardens, a vast park full of palm trees. Here, we stopped for a while to eat a couple of sandwiches that Yvonne had prepared with goodies from the breakfast buffet. Adel had brought his own lunch along plus some sweet Egyptian pastries which he offered us.

At this point, we chatted for a while and I asked him point blank why a highly educated gentleman such as himself was driving a cab.

"It is like this," he replied, "I enjoy being with English speaking tourists—Americans, English, anyone who speaks English. I can also speak French but not so well. I also enjoy showing tourists the sights of this great city."

"So have you been doing this all your working life?" I asked.

"Oh, no. I have been doing this for about six years. I used to work for an electronics plant for many years, about twenty. But then there was this layoff and everybody including supervisors like me were out the door, but we did receive a modest pension. I now add to that pension by being a tourist taxi driver. Also, I like the freedom. No more working indoors for me."

And with that, Adel said that we must forge ahead and take a look at Farouk's beachfront mansion, the Montazah Palace on the other side of the gardens. Even from a distance, it was quite impressive. It reminded me of the summer beach mansions in Newport, Rhode Island that once belonged to the super-rich.

**Montazah Palace**

Adel told us the palace was closed to the public so there was no opportunity to see its elegant interior. That was just as well since we were tired of palaces, temples and museums. All we wanted to see was the seafront. Adel then drove around and parked the car behind the palace. We got out and followed a boardwalk to the beach. Supposedly this beach, Mamoura Beach, was one of the best beaches in Alexandria. It was also a beach where women could wear skimpy bathing suits without being harassed.

Today, though the beach was nearly deserted and the sea choppy. Nonetheless, it was a nice relief from the city with all its congestion. We hung around for a while, snapped a few pictures and then left.

**Mamoura Beach**

**Allan & Yvonne**

By now it was approaching 3 p.m. and I could tell Adel was getting antsy and wanted to call it a day to beat the traffic going home. Yvonne and I were tired of sightseeing too but I wanted to see one last area of Alexandria, the oldest section in the city, the Anfushi district a mile beyond our hotel.

We had already passed by it yesterday when we visited the Citadel of Qaitbay but I wanted to see a few of the inner streets. Why? Most likely because that section was once home to Lawrence Durrell, the aforementioned author of the Alexandria Quartet. That is where he lived in the late 30s and early 40s as a minor official in the British Foreign Office. Of course in his Quartet, Durrell cast himself as a poor English school teacher he called Darby.

I already knew from my guide book that the Alexandria of that era had all but disappeared except for a few old landmarks like the Hotel Cecil and the Hotel Metropole where his fictional friend and novelist Percy Pursewarden lived. I also knew that the block that Durrell had lived on had been demolished and that in fact, the whole Anfushi area was undergoing renovation. Nonetheless, I wanted to see what remained.

So Adel drove back down the seafront boulevard, past the Cecil Hotel and down to the fish market. There he turned into a narrow street lined with slummy looking buildings replete with hanging laundry and TV satellite dishes.

**Anfushi District**

Really, there was not much to see here but the usual urban slum congestion with remarkable piles of uncollected garbage.

**Alexandrian Trash**

Of course no sign of Lawrence Durrell who died in 1990. But maybe his spirit lived on here, somewhere in this mess. Or least his description of Alexandria lives on:

> "Capitally, what is this city of ours? . .Alexandria? In a flash my mind's eye shows me a thousand dust tormented streets. Flies and beggars own it today and those who enjoy an intermediate existence. Five races, five languages, a dozen creeds: Five fleets turning through their greasy reflections behind the harbor bar...(T)here are more than five sexes and only the demotic Greek seems to distinguish among them. The sexual provender is staggering in its variety and profusion. You would never mistake it (Alexandria) for a happy place."

*Africa: Around the Edges*

**Laurence Durrell**

Following our quick look at Anfushi, Adel drove us back to Hotel Cecil where we rested for a couple of hours watching CNN International and then too tired to go out, we ordered room service for our dinner. Oh, by the way, we were looking forward to doing nothing the next day. Yvonne and I had decided to forgo sightseeing for a day of rest, our first real day of rest since this madcap, helter-skelter tour began over two weeks ago. When I informed Adel of this, he was disappointed saying he had a lot more to show us. I assured him we wanted his services Monday to go to El Alamein and then on Tuesday, to drive us to Cairo's International Airport where we would fly out the next day. He seemed happy with that and we departed on good terms.

**Sun. March 17**

About the only interesting thing we did the next day was to take a short walk around in our area observing the busy lives of Alexandrians as they went about their business. Note that Sunday is a regular workday in this Islamic country and everything was open. Meanwhile, my cold had come back and so one stop I made was at a little hole-in-the-wall pharmacy that carried cold pills.

Later we had coffee at the Hotel Metropole also on the square. Like Cecil, this hotel was one of the older ones still functioning in Alexandria with its own glorious history.

Built in 1902, it was home to many writers and artists including the Alexandrian poet Constantine Cavafy for twenty-five years. In contrast to the Cecil which had been somewhat modernized, the Metropole still retained the trappings of its original decor right down to the employee's period dress of the early 20th century. We thought that if we ever came to Alexandria again, we might stay here.

**Metropole Hotel**

*Africa: Around the Edges*

**Metropole Lounge**

That evening, we decided to sample one of the famous fish dishes of Alexandria. And while the favorite seafood restaurant in Alexandria, the Fish Market, was only about a mile away on the seafront boulevard, we settled for a fish dinner right in the hotel. We each had a large slab of grilled sea bass along with all the sides and a couple of Stella beers. Very fresh and tasty indeed. That was it. Tomorrow El Alamein.

# 15. EL ALAMEIN

**Mon. March 18**

The next morning we were out bright and early around 8 a.m. and there was Adel waiting to take us on our day trip to El Alamein about 120 kilometers west on the Mediterranean coast.

El Alamein? The battles of El Alamein? Does that ring a bell to anyone these days? Maybe to World War II history buffs knowledgeable about the North African campaigns and probably to many Egyptians because thanks to the British and other Commonwealth troops, they were saved from a German occupation of Egypt.

In fact, the approaching German and Italian troops from neighboring Libya inspired such fear that the British staff in Alexandria and Cairo were burning their documents and getting ready to evacuate Egypt. However, because the control of the Suez Canal was at stake, British and Commonwealth forces finally amassed under the leadership of Lieutenant-General Bernard Montgomery and then headed west to greet the Axis troops under the command of General Erwin Rommel in the fall of 1942. The result was a series of titanic battles near the tiny coastal town of El Alamein that left more than 90-thousand dead or wounded from both sides, but mostly from the Axis side. This battle site with all its attendant monuments, memorials and graves is where we were headed.

***

Once we got beyond the outskirts of Alexandria and into the desert countryside that extends along the whole northern coast of Egypt, we noticed on-going mega-developments, most of it resort development on the beachfront. One complex after another unfolded before our eyes with occasional glimpses of the blue Mediterranean beyond. Adel told us that these resort areas were mostly for the well-off from Cairo. It was their summer refuge since the temperatures were cooler here than those of sweltering Cairo.

**Sidi Abdel Rahman**

Here and there would be a new town development or a major expansion of an existing town like El Alamein.

**Downtown El Alamein**

Of course, the main reason for us being here in El Alamein was not the town but the war monuments. Our first stop at Adel's insistence was a surprise. It was, in fact, the German monument to its war dead in North Africa. And it was impressive indeed standing there on the coast looking like a medieval Turkish fortress.

**German War Memorial**

Inside, it was a revelation what with its circular courtyard and alcoves featuring an early Christian looking decoration and the carefully inscribed names of the 42-hundred war dead including a few Schusters, Yvonne's maiden name. This made sense because the Schusters originally came from Germany.

*Africa: Around the Edges*

**Coptic-like Icons**

**German War Dead**

**Schuster Dead**

Overall, an impressive monument to the German war dead. Yes, you could argue that the Germans were the enemy at the time, but a dead German soldier is the same as a dead Allied soldier. They are both dead and their friends and loved ones mourn alike. As usual, the German authorities did a good and efficient job of commemorating their soldiers.

Next, it was on to the Italian war monument commemorating the Italian soldiers that fought and died in North Africa. People forget that at that point in the war, Italy under Mussolini was allied with Germany. In addition, Italy effectively controlled Libya right next door to Egypt and had thousands of Italian troops stationed there. Thus it was that those Italian troops also fought bravely in the battle of El Alamein with some 48-hundred perishing. Hence their impressive monument.

*Africa: Around the Edges*

**Italian War Monument**

While striking looking from the outside, the interior of the memorial reminded me a Catholic Church with its stain glass windows and crosses everywhere.

**Church?**

And on the white marble walls that surrounded the interior, the names of the Italian dead were inscribed row after row. All in all, quite impressive.

Africa: Around the Edges

**Wall of the Fallen**

Last but not least, we headed over to the El-Alamein Military Museum and Commonwealth Cemetery. These were the good guys, the Brits, the Kiwis, the Aussies and a host of other Allied countries. For some reason, though, this whole complex was miles inland from the Mediterranean. In fact, it was located in a slightly seedy area on the outskirts of the town of El Alamein. O.K. Maybe land was cheap here.

So with a shrug, we sallied forth to see what we could see. After going through an admission gate, we came out onto a display ground of the military hardware used in the battle such as tanks, artillery, fighter planes, all arranged in various threatening positions.

## El-Alamein Military Museum

*Africa: Around the Edges*

After wandering around the grounds for while we went inside the museum proper and checked out the various exhibits. Aside from more weapons, military support gear and a gigantic battle map in the center of the museum, there in glassed-in displays were doughty Brit mannequins all dressed up in battle gear and ready to confront the enemy.

**El-Alamein Displays**

**Troops**

Other battle exhibits featured Australians, Canadians, New Zealanders and even the East Indians with a nod to the few Free French and Greeks that fought in this battle.

O.K. All very nice but where was the American exhibit? Looking around, I saw nothing. Weren't the Americans part of the Allies fighting the Germans in North Africa? Yes, but as I later learned, we had no ground troops participating in the battle of El Alamein. However, we did supply the Brits with Sherman tanks, bombers, fighter planes and other various weapons that ensured their victory. I thought at least we deserved an honorable mention but there was no mention of the American role anywhere in the museum. To the casual observer, it looked like an entirely a British Commonwealth show except for one lone soldier with a torch shoulder patch.

Actually, the US arrived rather late in the battles for North Africa. The Battle of El- Alamein was late summer and early fall in 1942. Americans didn't show up in force until November of 1942, in Operation Torch. Then we concentrated on French North Africa, mainly Morocco and Tunisia which bordered Libya.

It was in Tunisia that the U.S. Army encountered the Germans head to head in the battle of Kasserine Pass in late 1942 and were soundly defeated. Later in February of 1943, under General George Patton, the Americans finally prevailed. The Brits were also involved in that battle too. After an Allied victory there, Rommel, running out military resources, was forced to withdraw from North Africa.

Following the museum, we crossed the street and went over to inspect the Commonwealth Cemetery. Here we encountered row after row of headstones inscribed with the names of the fallen warriors.

*Africa: Around the Edges*

**Commonwealth War Cemetery**

I thought the cemetery was rather small compared to the military cemeteries I had seen once on the beaches of Normandy, France. But then a lot more troops had been killed there. At Alamein, the Allied Commonwealth dead numbered around 7,300.

Still, viewing these gravestones was a sobering experience. Most of them were for troops in their 20s, some in their early 30s, the typical cannon fodder age when wars are fought. However, World War II was considered the "good war," something worth fighting for. Then there was the "bad war," Vietnam.

I flashed back to that time of Vietnam when the mantra from many of the college twenty-somethings was "Hell no, we won't go." And most did not. Content with burning their draft cards, some escaped to Canada; others simply stayed in school getting student deferments until President Nixon abolished the draft in 1973. Others, like me, had joined the military reserves in 1964 before Vietnam got going. All I had to worry about was getting called up but that was a remote possibility since Johnson was reluctant to call on the reserves.

After going through this depressing cemetery, we called it a day for El Alamein. Adel, who had been waiting patiently by his cab while we visited the different sites, broke out in a big grin when we indicated we were ready to go back to Alexandria.

That night we had a quick pizza dinner to go from our nearby restaurant. This time we had a couple of Stella beers and ate the pizza in our room. That was it for Alexandria. Tomorrow back to Cairo for one night at a hotel near the International Airport and then on Wednesday, homeward.

# 16. HOMEWARD

**Tue. March 19**

This was the day to say goodbye to Alexandria. We felt we had seen enough although we knew there was plenty more to see. Most international visitors to Egypt only spend a day here enduring a five hour round trip by car, train, or tour bus from Cairo. It's a long exhausting day where you only see a few of the highlights of this city. Alexandria deserves much more than that and I felt our four-day stay here did it justice.

Anyway, we bid Mohammad goodbye, giving him a twenty-dollar tip for which he seemed grateful. But then he asked me to give him a mention on Trip Advisor as being an excellent person to arrange personal tours of Alexandria. I said I certainly would. And back home, I did.

Meanwhile, Adel loaded our suitcases on the carrier rack on top of his car while I looked on frowning. Seeing my concern, Adel assured me that the luggage was very secure on top since he had tied them down well. I still would have preferred them in the trunk. End the end, he was right. The luggage stayed secured on top.

Around nine, we finally started on our long drive back to Cairo. Although the weather was great, it promised to be a long, boring drive. I was in the front seat with Adel; Yvonne was in the back seat where she promptly fell asleep. I tried to read but with all the motion of the car in traffic, that was impossible. So Adel and I made small talk.

He talked about his family, his wife and his two grown sons, one of whom was now going to university to study engineering and who also wanted to work abroad in Europe or maybe in the U.S. since wages were so low in Egypt and jobs were scarce. I mentioned what El-Sisi was trying to do to encourage industry and building infrastructure.

"There should be plenty of jobs connected with that," I observed.

"Yes," replied Adel and then added, "if you know the right people and have the right connections. That's the way Egypt operates."

End of discussion.

\*\*\*

Once out into the marsh and desert country, we began to clip along, stopping about a halfway through for a bathroom break and a snack. Adel opened his trunk and pulled out a box of baked goods prepared by his wife and offered us some. These were delicious little squares of honey and rice and who knows what else and these goodies along with some hot tea from a large thermos that Adel had, we had a little mid-morning snack.

After about another hour and a half more of seeing the same sights we saw a few days ago in reverse, we entered the outskirts of Cairo and took an expressway cutoff to the airport.

Soon we approached the entrance of the airport and I directed Adel to the Meridian Airport Hotel. He nodded as if he knew where it was but after a while, I noticed that he wasn't going into the airport proper. Now I had seen this hotel when we first arrived in Egypt. It was right next to the International Terminal. I mentioned this to Adel but he was adamant he knew how to get there. Indeed, we did arrive at a Meridian hotel. I was confused when we saw the sign. I protested to Adel that this Meridian wasn't the right one.

Apparently not believing me, Adel shrugged, got out of the car and talked to the doorman and then he turned and came back sheepishly saying, "You are right Mr. Brown. This is not the right one. There are two Meridian Hotels at the airport. This is the old one; the new one is right near the International Terminal."

No shit, I thought. What a waste of time since Adel was so bullheaded and didn't listen to me. Anyway, we made it over to the main airport entrance where Adel had to pay a parking admission fee much to his disgust. Off in the distance, we could see the new Meridian Hotel all sleek and gleaming in the afternoon sunlight right where I said it would be.

So he drove over. The hotel security guards checked us out and then raised the gate so we could park in front of the entrance. I hustled ahead to the check-in desk to verify our reservations.

Meanwhile, Adel unloaded our luggage and then stood around obviously waiting for his payoff but also making a call on his cell phone. While I was temporarily pissed off at him for being so headstrong in finding this hotel, Adel was actually a great guy and had given us a great tour of Alexandria, El Alamein and a safe drive to the airport. So I peeled off a hundred dollar bill US his stated fee for driving us here and then I added another fifty US dollars for a tip. Adel then broke into a big smile and shook my hand, saying, "Now I can buy more gas."

He turned and hugged Yvonne and then announced that he had found a fare to take back to Alexandria. So after all, this had been a red letter day for Adel making him even more money. We were happy for him and sorry to see him go but he did give me his card and asked me to give him a good review on Trip Advisor. I said I would and I did. And that was the last that we saw of Adel as he drove off with his new fare, a well-turned-out older woman.

Yvonne and I made our way into this very sleek and modern hotel and took the elevator up to our room, a luxurious room for a modest price of only 120 US. After we were settled, I explored around a bit and discovered that on the third floor there was a rampway right into the International Terminal. Talk about convenience. This was the ultimate for catching an early flight home. We could just roll out of bed and take a short walk to the check-in desk for our 7:30 a.m. Lufthansa flight tomorrow. Of course, that meant going to bed early.

So while taking all of this in, I retired to the downstairs bar and had a much deserved Stella thinking how I was going to miss this beer. Later, we ordered room service for dinner and retired early.

## Wed. March 20

Early the next morning around 5 a.m., we packed up and headed down the 3rd floor rampway to the International Terminal with one of the bell boys rolling our luggage along on a cart. Check-in was quick and easy and a couple of hours later we were winging our way back to Munich. There we would have a quick change of planes and would continue our journey to Denver.

And that was the end of Egypt for us and the end of this story. Would we ever come back to Egypt? Not likely but then you never know. There is still a lot more to see. Stay tuned.

**FIN**

# APPENDIX

### EGYPTIAN DYNASTIES/KINGDOMS

Here is a rough guide to six thousand years of ancient Egyptian history based on Jason Thompson's **History of Egypt.**

1. **PREDYNASTIC PERIOD 6000—2950 BC**
    a. NABTA Period 6000 BC: Neolithic existence in western Egypt which ended with desert encroachment. Moved to the Nile.
    b. Baradian period 4400—4000 BC: origin of Egyptian culture
    c. Nagada period 4000—3000 BC: unification of Egypt

2. **EARLY DYNASTIC 2950--2613 BC**
    a. Djoser: Built Saqqara Step Pyramid 2686 BC: beginning of pyramid building in Memphis.
    b. Architect/Visor/Imhotep. 2686 BC

3. **OLD KINGDOM 2613—2160 BC**
    a. A time of culture, order, self-sufficiency in isolation. The pharaoh was considered a God King whose function was to dispense Maat: order, truth, justice. Also developed was a system of taxation/scribal literacy and hieroglyphs.
    b. Sneferu: (2613 BC) first great builder of classic pyramids. Built three. Bent, Red, Northern

c. Khufu (Cheops) Sneferu's son built the Great Pyramid. (2590—2540 BC) maybe by dragging huge blocks of limestone stones up earthen ramps.

d. Khafre (son of Khufu) was possible the model of Sphinx head. (c. 2500 BC)

e. Pepy II: longest ruler in Old Kingdom (2278-2184) Warrior. With his death, end of Old Kingdom

f. Main Gods: Osiris, a primeval king of Egypt, Isis, wife of Osiris, mother of Horus the falcon-headed god, Sobek (crocodile).

4. **FIRST INTERMEDIATE PERIOD 2160—2055 BC**
A time of chaos, war anarchy and poverty.

5. **MIDDLE KINGDOM 2055—1640 BC**

   a. Noted for realistic statues, new architectural designs, new art and literary works.

   b. Mentuhotep II (2055 BC) Reign lasted 50 years, restored order, finances, trade with middle east, built infrastructure, canals, irrigation, etc. Capital of Egypt, Thebes

   c. Amenemhet I (1985 BC) Visor who seized throne. Built chintzy pyramids, Warrior

   d. Construction of Temple of Amada in Nubia (c.1850 BC) under Amenemhet II

   e. Amenemhet III (1831-1786 BC) reached cultural apex, Egypt peaceful and prosperous.

6. **SECOND INTERMEDIATE PERIOD 1640—1550 BC**

   a. Period of foreign Invasion and rule by the Hyksos, mostly Canaanites from the east. Some Egyptologist say it was a gradual invasion over several hundred years, mostly peaceful and that it was punctuated by Hyksos being chased out at various points which may have given rise to the great Exodus myth led by a mythical Moses. Also, note that the Israelites/Canaanites also wandered in and out of Egypt over a period of hundreds of years.

*Africa: Around the Edges*

    b. Hyksos brought new technology: potter wheel, loom, horse-drawn chariots, curved sword, compound bows, body armor

7. **NEW KINGDOM 1550--1069 BC**
   a. Hatshesput (1473-58) woman ruler: well run reign
   b. Supposedly, Israelites exodus from Egypt during reign of co-regency of Tuthmoses III, 1446 BC.
   Son Amenhotep I.
   c. Amenhotep II, III, 1425-1352 BC victory in war, peace and prosperity. Started building Monuments at Karnak & Luxor.
   d. Akhenaten (1352 BC) established new, supreme sun god Aten and new capital, Amarna. Wife Nefertiti (1350), son Tutankhaten.
   e. Tutankhaten (boy king) rules for ten years, (1332 –1323 BC) is wounded and dies. Egypt goes back to original gods.
   f. Ramses II (1279 BC) great warrior and continues building Karnak. Battle of Kadesh.
   g. Temple Abu Simbel (1264 BC) built by Ramses, Luxor.
   h. Valley of Kings established due to pyramid robbers.

8. **THIRD INTERMEDIATE PERIOD 1069-715 BC**
   a. Libyans take over, leader Shosheng (945) defeats Kingdom of Judah and Israel following death of Solomon.
   b. Kingdom of Kush (770) Nubians take over upper Egypt

9. **LATE PERIOD 715—31 BC**
   a. Ptolemies from Greece take over (305 BC—31 AD)
   b. Temples of Philae (c. 380 BC)
   c. Dakka Temple (c. 300 BC) Greco-Roman temple in Nubia. Dedicated to Troth, god of wisdom.
   d. Temple of Horus (Edfu) (c. 273 BC)
   e. Kom Ombo Temple 180 BC double temple dedicated to Sobek the crocodile god, and Horus the falcon-headed god.

f. New Kalabsha Temple 30BC. The temple was a tribute to Mandulis a Lower Nubian sun god
   g. Cleopatra VII/Mark Anthony 45-30 BC

**Christian Period:**

Christianity introduced to Egypt during reign of Nero (50 AD) by St. Mark. Possible reason for adoption: Osiris, Isis and Horus could be taken as allegory of the Holy family. Osiris presumably God, Isis equated to Mary, her son Horus equated to Jesus. The pharaoh was also considered the incarnate son of God.

# Upper Egypt Temples

Abu Simbel
The Great Temple

Abu Simbel
The Small Temple

**Abu Simbel**

www.ingramcontent.com/pod-product-compliance
Lightning Source LLC
Chambersburg PA
CBHW05083523 0426
43667CB00012B/2010